Coping With EXAMS and TESTS

PETER COREY
illustrated by
Philip Reeve

Hippo

This book is dedicated to anyone who has ever had to eat an entire biro during an exam, just for something to do.

Scholastic Children's Books
Commonwealth House, 1-19 New Oxford Street
London WC1A 1NU, UK

A division of Scholastic Ltd
London ~ New York ~ Toronto ~ Sydney ~ Auckland

First published by Scholastic Ltd, 1998

ISBN 0 590 19683 9

Typeset by TW Typesetting, Midsomer Norton, Somerset

Printed by Cox & Wyman Ltd, Reading, Berks.

Contents

DO YOU NEED THIS BOOK?

In order to help you decide, try this simple test:
1) Can you read?[1]
2) Do you like books, even when they suddenly force you to laugh out loud in front of total strangers?
3) Do you hate exams?
4) Have you got some spare cash lying around in your pocket?
5) Can you say: "Excuse me, Mr/Mrs Bookshop Person, I would like to purchase this extremely fine and hilarious book by the multi-award winning[2] author Peter Corey, who is apparently not only unbelievably talented, but also a thoroughly nice bloke to boot"?

Stand on your head for the answers.

How did you do?
The answers you were looking for are:
1) Yes
2) Er … yes
3) Most definitely!
4) Hang on, I'll check … just about
5) Easily

If you got all of the answers correct, this book is for you. If you got most of them right, it's still likely to be up your street. Most or all answers wrong? Buy the book anyway! Who knows, it might improve your brain-power. It'll certainly improve the conduction of your chuckle muscles. So off you go and buy it. I'll meet you over the page once you've paid for it.

1: If you understood the question then the answer is almost certainly "yes".
2: The *Coping With…* books have inspired TV programmes, which so far have won nine BAFTAs, and loads of other awards.

Book owners start here

Congratulations! You are now the proud owner of the latest *Coping With...* book. If you haven't bought this book but are still reading it, then put it down at once! This is not a library, you know![1]

Within the pages of this book is everything you'll ever need to know – and some stuff that you'll *never* need to know – about exams, tests and any other situation where some total stranger starts poking about in the contents of your brain with a dirty stick. It will show you how to deal with the stress of exams and tests, how to prepare for them, and even how to cheat! But first...

As you might imagine with a book about exams, there are a few pre-reading rules that must be observed. Eating, drinking[2] and sleeping will not be permitted during the reading of this book. Anyone caught with a bag of sweets whilst reading will be made to share them round. If the book is being read by more than one person at the same time, then the passing of notes is

---

1: If you *are* reading this book in a library, then please accept my apologies.
2: Well OK you can eat and drink if you like – but don't spill it on any of the funny bits.

strictly forbidden. Also, no help must be offered with the long words.

Anyone caught breaking any of these rules will have the book confiscated, and be forced to read *Fun With Algebra* Volumes 1–37 instead. You may have as long as you like to complete the book, and may even take it into the lavatory with you. You may now turn over the page and begin reading.

Testing, Testing

Imagine the situation: there you are, palms sweating, head buzzing, sitting in rows with most of your mates, and you haven't the foggiest idea what to do next. This is one situation where your pals can't help you. You've got to crack this one alone.

No, I'm not referring to a heavy date at the movies with Melanie Dipstick or Colin Wingnutt, although the situation is a bit similar – certainly the sweaty palms and not knowing what to do next. I'm talking about an exam. Exams and tests are probably the most stressful things that you'll have to face in the first 20 or so years of your life. Obviously there are other stressful situations (meeting your girlfriend's parents, meeting your boyfriend's girlfriend, etc.), but the most stressful involves the answering of questions, usually questions that you don't even understand, let alone know the answer to! And when you've answered these questions, or tried to, one question (which has not been asked) remains unanswered:

WHAT THE HECK WAS ALL THAT ABOUT?

It's easy to imagine that there is no good reason for exams and tests or that the only reason is to make your life as miserable as possible. Although this is very likely, it can't be the whole answer. Why not? Well, mainly because the organizing of exams and tests – setting up, marking, etc. – is every bit as painful as actually doing them. Adults may be stupid,[1] but even they wouldn't put themselves through all that pain for no reason at all. So what are exams for? A way of finding out *whether things are as they should be*.

1: Actually there's no "may be" about it. They *are* stupid!

To try and explain this I'll give you a simple example. A spelling test is used to test whether you know certain spellings. Why? Because the teacher whose job it is to make sure that you know those spellings might get asked about it by somebody; the head teacher or an OFSTED[1] inspector might say to them: "Can your class spell such and such a word?"

"Yes," says the teacher.

"Prove it!" says the inspector.

"Here are the results of a recent spelling test," says the smarty-pants teacher.

"Oh," says the inspector, and makes a mental note to try and catch the teacher out over something else.

Of course the thing that's unfair in all this is the fact that you have had to do the test in the first place. Wouldn't it have been better for the inspector to ask *you* if you knew the words? But that would be too simple. No one would have suffered.

An alternative would be for the teacher to be tortured in increasingly painful and interesting ways until they confessed that you knew the spellings.

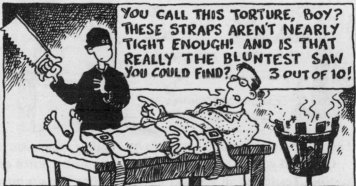

YOU CALL THIS TORTURE, BOY? THESE STRAPS AREN'T NEARLY TIGHT ENOUGH! AND IS THAT REALLY THE BLUNTEST SAW YOU COULD FIND? 3 OUT OF 10!

Again this method is flawed – the teacher could be lying; the teacher might die before the inspector got any

1: Which stands for the OFfice of STandards in EDucation. Or something.

kind of sensible answer out of them;[1] the teacher might never reply because they were enjoying the torture too much. That would never do, even though pain is an essential part of the examination process. No – the best solution all round is to test *you*.

I say "the best solution all round", but it isn't the best solution for you, because you're the one doing the test. But – as we will discover – your feelings are not being considered by anybody, least of all those people who devise the various exams and tests.

Your starter for ten

This is the traditional way in which a new section of questions is started on *University Challenge*, a TV programme in which two groups of university students are given a test disguised as a game show. The added problem for one of the teams is that they have to balance the other team on their heads for the entire programme – presumably they lost the toss. The team on top have the disadvantage of being two metres up in the air.

I suppose this is what they mean by "higher education".

Quiz and game shows are in fact just another form of testing. Testing is all around us all the time. I'll go into this is much greater detail later, but let's first try to answer the question…

1: As you know teachers never give sensible answers.

How did it Start?

Exams and tests are not things that were dreamt up a few years ago. They have been around since the dawn of time. Oh yes, they might have got more sophisticated over the years – they might even have got harder – but the basic principle of testing as a form of discovering something has always been with us. To understand how it has developed we firstly have to realize that testing develops from natural curiosity. The process works (or doesn't work) something like this:

Curiosity leads to exploration – firstly exploration of the environment, then of the other things in the environment, then of the other creatures in the environment. This then leads to *comparison*: is this object bigger/smaller/tastier than I am? Is this other creature bigger/smaller/tastier than I am? This leads to *testing*. So, let's sum it up this way:

And then testing leads to exams. Wouldn't you just know it!

To understand how all this works in practice we need to trek back through the dusty corridors of time, avoiding the bigger cobwebs and nastier dribblings underfoot, to … er … *examine* the roots of testing. Ready to be amazed? Good. You may now begin.

DYATHINKISAURUS?

Dinosaurs were not the least bit curious. This is probably why they died out – they weren't the least bit bothered about exploring their environment, trying new foods, inventing the wheel and so forth. The bigger dinosaurs ate the leaves at the tops of trees because that's what they bumped into as they lumbered around the primeval swamp. Tyrannosaurus Rex, a smaller dinosaur with a big mouth and too many teeth, loved charging around snapping his jaws.[1] Naturally anything that got in his way (usually other dinosaurs) got eaten. How was he to know that he was actually a vegetarian (if indeed he was)? It never occurred to him to find out. He never stopped charging around long enough to say to himself: "D'you know, if I was to get a couple of tree trunks, some sturdy branches and a few metres of vine I could make myself a ladder, climb up that tree, and get a handful of those leaves. I wonder what they taste

1: With a name like that he was destined to be a bully.

like?" T. Rex had no thirst for knowledge – he was too busy eating other dinosaurs.

The notions of testing or examination were as alien to the average dinosaur as Fred Flintstone was. It wasn't until man (and woman) walked the earth that *curiosity* was born. And as we all know that *curiosity* – the root of all forms of examination and testing – killed the cat. But then if it hadn't, the cat would probably have been eaten by a dinosaur anyway.

ONE MAN AND HIS BRAIN

Without curiosity we would probably all still be living in caves, grabbing our lunch as it went past on its way to the nearest water hole, and not even giving a second's thought as to what to watch on TV. But from the first moment that Early Person said to himself: "I wonder what would happen if I hit myself with this rock?" the idea of testing and examination was born. It would have been better if Early Person had killed himself with the rock. Instead of which he merely gave himself a) a terrible headache, and b) a terrible thirst for knowledge. This is how such things work:

1) Early Person picks up a rock and says: "I wonder what will happen ... etc."

2) Early Person then whacks himself firmly over the head with said rock.

3) Early Person passes out.

4) Early Person wakes up again, only to find that his favourite Pointy Stick is missing (pinched by a passing pointy-stick burglar), and has been replaced by a splitting headache. Early Person concludes: "Rock + Head = Loss of Pointy Stick + Gain of Splitting Headache". Or, to put it in equation form:

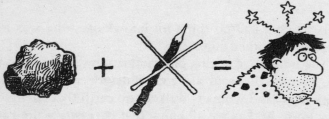

Now that would be enough for most of us – especially the headache part. But not Early Person. Early Person now wants to know whether the *size* of the rock has any effect on the disappearance of the stick. Early Person creates a series of tests involving larger and larger rocks, producing bigger and bigger headaches and the loss of a wider and wider range of useful household items. Thus the idea of *comparison* is born. The rock experiment was developed to include other Early Persons. How would a range of rocks affect a range of heads? And what about other animals? Yes, they had animal testing even then! Not that too many Early

Persons complained about that, because they knew that if they were to stop the animals being hit around the head, they'd have to suffer it themselves. After all, this was vital research for the good of Person-kind, wasn't it?

Good, Better, Best...

Next came competition. It was the ancient Greeks who invented the Olympic Games, or *Blokes Running About With Nothing On*, as it was originally called. The idea of the Games was to test Man's physical strength and prowess, as well as his ability to withstand girls pointing at his bottom and laughing.

I WISH SOMEBODY WOULD HURRY UP AND INVENT THE SACK RACE...

Little can the ancient Greeks have realized what they were starting. If they'd known that several centuries later the Olympics would be more about sponsorship than sport, would they still have gone ahead? Who knows? All we can be sure of is that something that was started as a bit of fun – rather like World War I – did much to kindle the spirit of competition that was eventually to turn natural curiosity and a need to explore and compare things into the examination system that underpins the whole of today's society.[1]

1: Unlike World War I.

Golden boy-Golden Fleece

Of course these ancient civilizations had their share of tests and exams even then, but they took the form of *quests*. A quest is basically a test, but it doesn't usually involve writing, which is handy because a lot of the early heroes were none too hot on the old joined-up biro waggling. Take Jason, for instance. He was given the task of finding the Golden Fleece. The only clue they gave him was that it was on a golden ram (probably) – although by the time he found it, it might have been in an Oxfam shop. Because the trouble was that Jason didn't go straight there, mainly because he didn't know where "there" was.

Eventually Jason found the fleece and took it back home. But the big question is – why? What good did it do him? Did it help him in the thrustingly competitive job market that was ancient Greece? Of course it didn't!

"Our Wayne's got nine GSCEs and six GBHNVQs"

"Really? Well, our Jason's got a golden fleece."

Not surprisingly, Jason ended up cleaning chariot windscreens as they stopped at the traffic lights – with a bucket of soapy water and lump of Golden Fleece, naturally!

Knight and day

Other early western civilizations – which actually weren't civilized at all – had their own method of sorting the best from the rest. Again there was no written test, let alone a spot of French oral. And again they took the form of quests. Take King Arthur, for example. How did he become king? Did he have to sit an exam? Did he have to examine – in no less than 3,000 words – the use of metaphor in the writings of Emily Brontë? No. All he had to do was pull a sword out of a stone. He didn't even have to put forward a theory to attempt to explain how the sword got there in the first place.

Once he became king he continued this fine tradition of testing, although I think this was due more to his lack of mathematical skill than anything else. Let me explain. The first thing Arthur did when he became king was to build a fine palace (as you do) and invite all the best knights from the four corners of the Earth[1] to sit at his table. In fact he had a table built specially, but a big round one. Not big enough, as it turned out, but then Arthur knew nothing of maths. He couldn't even begin to calculate the knight to table-space ratio, multiply it by shepherd's pie-r-squared, and take away the number you first thought of. Not that he was an uneducated man – he wasn't. He had his own tutor (Merlin the Magician) who taught him spelling – or rather doing spells. Arthur was a keen student, and in a matter of months he could turn a frog into an individual frog pie,

1: They thought the Earth was square in those days.

which is not a lot of use when you've got a hundred hungry knights to feed.

HE'S STILL HAVING TROUBLE WITH THIS KNIGHT-TO-TABLE RATIO...

So it was a case of learning more impressive cookery spells or setting harder and harder tests to limit the number of knights who came to lunch. Arthur chose the latter, having learned nothing from the experiences of the ancient civilizations. Not that Arthur even knew about the Greeks and Egyptians – you see, education at this point was rather on a "need to know" basis. It was only really the monks and other churchmen who needed a solid education. Why? Because they were translating the Bible so that other people could read it. What other people? Er ... well nobody at that point, but the monks didn't realize that until they'd done it.

Anyway, back to King Arthur. In order to work out which knights were fit to sit at the round table he came up with more and more difficult tests.

Arthur's favourite quest was "find the Holy Grail". For those of you who don't know, this was the goblet that Christ had supposedly drunk out of at the Last Supper. Well, frankly it might have been anywhere (except in the dishwasher if they had any sense, because everybody knows that dishwashers are really bad for silver, despite what the adverts say). But the quests, even if they were completed, were fairly useless. So you got to sit at Arthur's round table! Big deal! You got to eat his individual frog pie, which was hardly a meal – more of a snack. You also got to listen to all the other knights banging on about their latest quest…

…AND SO I SLEW THE MAIDEN AND UNTIED THE DRAGON. I THINK THAT'S WHAT HAPPENED…

YAWN

ZZZ

I'M OFF!

And if you were really unlucky you got to watch Arthur doing his latest magic trick, which in those days usually involved three cups and a ball.[1] Again the testing and questing had no practical purpose, but that didn't stop them doing it.

killing me softly with his lance

The Age of Chivalry was a great time to be a woman. Most men thought so, anyway. Whether women would actually agree is another matter. The men spent their days charging around on horseback trying to jab each other with a 30-foot stick. Why? Why not! Actually it was to see who could stay on their horse the longest. This is an obvious forerunner of today's "laddish" contests – who can pee the highest, walk backwards the furthest, knock on the most doors and run away the quickest. None of it had (or even has) any practical use, other than proving that some people are better at it than others. The notion of testing was by now a firm part of the world's culture, but finding a practical application for that testing was still a long way off.

1: This particular trick is so old that even the ancient Egyptians knew it. But nobody was going to tell Arthur that!

Which witch is witch?

By the Middle Ages everyone had got the testing bug. There were tests for everything – "Will my bullock go faster if I poke it with a stick?" "Will my goat yield more milk if I threaten it with a rolled-up newspaper?" etc., etc. These tests were fairly harmless (unless you happened to be a goat or a bullock). It was when tests started to spread to humans that the trouble started.

In Medieval times people were very superstitious. Religion was fairly new and they hadn't quite got the hang of it. All they knew was that certain things that had been totally acceptable since Adam was a boy were now suddenly evil. Strapping a toad to your head to cure warts or shoving a newt up your nose to cure hay fever had been tried and tested for centuries, but because they weren't mentioned in the Bible (although they might have got lost in the translation) they were no longer allowed. Superstition bred fear, and fear bred prejudice, as it does.

Old Mother Wibley, who had been dispensing homeopathic cures all her life, was suddenly the sister of the Devil and branded a witch, even though nobody really knew what one was. Well, nobody except Malcolm Parsley, the self-styled Witchfinder General. But you couldn't condemn somebody as a witch without the proper testing, even in those days. Testing was by now the popular way of determining everything, not least witches. Besides, it all added to the spectacle, and since Malcolm was charging five groats a witch, people wanted their money's worth.

There were various degrees of witch testing, depending on how much you wanted to pay. For a penny, for instance, you could have the straightforward "Are you a witch?" test. This was rarely very satisfactory because most potential witches answered "No", whether they understood

20

the question or not.[1] For three pence there was the "If we let you go, will you confess to being a witch?" test. This caught out a surprisingly large number of innocent women. For four pence you could have the "threatening with something a bit smelly" test and so on right up to the "trial by ducking stool" – which cost a month's wages and was a bit of a non-event unless your village had a decent-sized river. The way this particular test worked was thus: you tied the suspect witch to a stool on the end of a pole and dipped the pole in a river. If the woman drowned she was innocent (but dead) and if she lived she was guilty and you burned her at the stake.

"Cruel but fair," according to Malcolm Parsley, who made his fortune and retired to the Lake District, where he set up a reflexology clinic.[2]

1: The basic rule in medieval times was "Say no to everything. You'll get the thumb-screws anyway." This was known as the "rule of thumb".
2: He discovered reflexology by accident, or rather by stepping on a nail.

The Age of Discovery

As the known world grew and countries started trading with each other (as well as killing each other) the need to be more competitive became a must. As trade grew, so did culture and discovery. Transport needed to be faster and faster and many people rose to the challenge. Leonardo da Vinci invented the helicopter, but it wasn't a lot of use because nobody had invented the helipad or the air-sea rescue service. But new inventions were coming along every day, all inspired by a spirit of curiosity, exploration and comparison – the same spirit that would eventually be the root of all testing and examination, and the basis of education. Unfortunately the masses had no use for these inventions, because they had no education. It was time to get them to…

Sit up straight!

It wasn't until education became available to the masses (and not just the rich) that testing and examination found its proper niche – if indeed it actually has one. As I've already said the clergy needed to be educated so that they could translate the Bible – and other books – into a language that everyone could understand, i.e. something other than Latin! Once they had finished all this translating they turned around and said:

22

And so the monks set about educating people in order that they could read the books that the monks had carefully translated from Latin. What do you think the monks did by way of education? That's right! They taught everybody Latin! So everybody could now read the *original* books (i.e. before they'd been translated). Smart or what? "What", actually. But then that's the nature of education: teach people the very thing they don't need to know and test them mercilessly about it! Even in Shakespeare's day children hated school.[1] And they hated testing even more. And why? Because *tests are not natural.*

Now you might be saying: "Hang on! You've just explained (at some length) how testing has developed steadily over the centuries!" I know, but that still doesn't mean that it's natural. And it isn't. Curiosity is natural, exploration is natural, but testing and examination aren't. So why do we bother with it? To try and explain that, let's look at it in more detail. To do that we need to go back to the drawing board – or rather the blackboard.

1: Mind you I'm not surprised if they had to go to school with him. He probably bored everybody to death by telling them the plot of his latest play.

Examining the tests

As soon as school became the norm for most children it became obvious that some method of judging whether or not the pupils were learning anything had to be introduced. After all, many of the early teachers were just ex-pupils who had never worked out where the exit door was. There was really nothing to say that they would be able to teach. In fact many of them couldn't, which is why people became concerned enough to want to introduce some method of checking whether or not the pupils were learning anything.

Now I think we'd all agree that that's fair enough. The idea that pupils should be checked in some way to make sure that the stuff they're being taught is going in one ear and staying there seems to me to be a quite reasonable one – or at least it would be if it stopped there. But of course it didn't, and doesn't. If anything it's got much, much worse. Remember that in Shakespeare's day there were no OFSTED inspectors. The only figure of school authority (apart from the teacher) was probably the bloke who came round to make sure that you were still chained to your desk properly.

The most extreme test you were subjected to would be a bit of Latin which, considering that's pretty well all they taught, was not too bad a prospect at all. These days, with anything up to about 50 different subjects to choose from, the potential for testing and exams is endless! And of course it doesn't end with school. Testing and exams have managed to infiltrate every possible corner of our lives. But where does it all start?

Putting us to the test

Almost from the moment we're born, somebody wants to test us. Even as we enter the world, some silly doctor dangles us upside down to see if we cry, which of course we do. But as a newborn baby you don't know any different, so if somebody wearing a white coat and smelling of soap comes up and starts shining a torch up your nose, you just assume that this is the kind of stuff that happens in *the world outside the womb*.

The first test that babies undergo (after the crying one) is the test to make sure they've got all the bits they should have and none of the bits they shouldn't have. A doctor (with certificates to prove that he's done the necessary exams to be able to carry out this job) checks them off, on a checklist not surprisingly. He also has a picture of a baby to help him decide whether two is the right number of legs or not. This done, the baby is left alone almost long enough to be able to drop off to sleep, when another doctor arrives to check that the baby has all the normal functions that a baby should have.

"Does Baby[1] sleep?" asks the doctor.

"He might if you left him alone long enough," replies the stressed-out mum.

The doctor then performs a number of tests, including tapping the infant on the knee with a hammer. This is apparently to check whether or not the baby reacts normally to ... er ... being tapped on the knee with a hammer. Now I don't know about you, but my normal reaction to being hit anywhere with a hammer (even by a doctor) would probably be: "Try that again, Face-ache, and you'll get a thick ear!" Surprisingly very few babies have been known to respond in this way, and yet most doctors record their reaction as "normal".

1: They never seem capable of saying the baby's name.

Eventually the baby is allowed to go home, but not until it has been weighed many, many times, presumably to test the scales.

Once at home you might imagine that the poor little baby might get a rest from testing. But oh no! There's the hearing test, which can take place when the poor kid is only about eight months old, far too young to be able to say, "I don't fancy it, thanks very much."

Of course the problem with a lot of these tests is that they are comparative. By that I mean that somebody has decided at some point that at a certain age a baby should be able to smile, talk, burp, fart, whatever. Any baby that can't do these things must therefore have something wrong with it. But not all babies are the same. Like all humans they develop at different rates, which is where all testing falls down. But that doesn't stop the testers carrying on with it. And the minute the poor thing sets foot inside a school the whole thing really gets going in earnest.

Seat of learning – source of testing

As we'll discover later, school is not the only area where testing and exams impinge on our lives. But it is the key one, mainly because we spend most of our working day there, and it provides us with the qualifications (or not!) that we need (or not!) in the Big Wide World. Testing and exams play a major role in school life, a role that, since the introduction of the National Curriculum,[1] has increased considerably, not only for the pupils but also for the teachers.

Nevertheless it's hard to believe, when you first start school, that the teachers are interested in anything other than making your life as pleasant as possible. OK, so they send home the occasional list of spellings, but

1: Covered in greater detail in the A–Z section. I bet you can't wait!

nothing too hard. Even your mum can do some of them. But you are still being tested, without knowing it.

You see at infant level the testing is done with such subtlety that it would make even a ninja's eyes water. You think nothing of it when the teacher asks you a seemingly innocent question:

Little do you realize as she fondly watches you half-killing yourself on the Big Gym Apparatus that you are being constantly assessed. Yes, that nice lady in the Fairisle sweater knows exactly how you're doing at Key Stage One.[1]

Of course there is the occasional formal test, but these tend to be disguised as fund-raising events. I'm talking about sponsored spells and that sort of thing. In fact it's possible to go all the way through your infant school education believing that the hardest thing you

1: Key Stage One? This is part of the National Curriculum in England, Wales and Northern Ireland. In Scotland the key stages are known as Level A, B, C etc. In both places they're also known as a pain in the butt! See the section on National Curriculum in the A–Z for a fuller explanation.

ever had to do was play the recorder – if you don't count having to share the Lego. Or at least it would be, apart from one thing: SATs.

"What are they?" I hear you ask, because you've probably heard of them, you've almost certainly done them, but you probably never really knew exactly what they were. Well, never fear – I'll tell you. SATs are Statutory Attainment Targets, an essential part of the National Curriculum. A team of so-called "experts" has sat down and worked out what they believe your average child (although there's no such thing) should be able to do at a certain age. So for instance they might say that the average seven-year-old should be able to write their name in joined-up writing, juggle and know the capital of China. Something like that.

HOW MANY MORE TIMES PATSY? YOU'RE NOT SUPPOSED TO BE ABLE TO BUILD A LUNAR MODULE UNTIL YOU'RE NINE

These targets form the basis of league tables, which are the way in which schools (not pupils) are tested to see how well they're doing.[1] That's the theory anyway. In practice the league tables don't actually tell you anything at all,[2] but that doesn't stop them being published.

The only people who are really affected by SATs are you, because you have to do them. Oh, and teachers, because they have to organize them – but you don't want to start feeling sorry for teachers, do you? Neither

1: League tables are explained more fully in the A–Z.
2: More of this later.

do I! But how do SATs actually work? Well, there are two bits – the teacher assessment, which is based on your work in class, and a written test. The two lots of results are then sent away to be studied by "experts", the two separate bits are compared, and the results are worked out. The problem from a teacher's point of view is a three-part one:

1) If the children do much worse in the teacher assessment bit of the test than they do in the written part, everyone will say that the teachers don't realize how clever their pupils are.

2) If the children do a lot *better* in the teacher assessment than they do in the written bit, people will say that the teachers don't realize how stupid their pupils are, or that the teachers are making it up.

3) If the children do badly in both tests, people will say that the teachers don't know how to teach.[1]

Either way the teachers can't win. But then that's their problem. Your problem is having to do the test in the first place. Although if you're an infant you probably won't even know it's happening. You might think it's odd that you're doing work and your teacher says she can't help you; you might think it's odd that she's got more steam coming out of her ears than normal, but you won't realize (probably) that you're being tested. This is because teachers, by and large, decide not to tell infants that it's happening. But then this test (important though it might be for somebody) is small fry compared with stuff that comes up later. In fact the minute you get to juniors things start to hot up, even if your love life takes a nosedive.

From mixed infant to mixed-up junior

Testing, as I've already said several times, is a means of determining what level people are achieving and, in the

1: Incidentally if the pupils do very well in both tests, people will still blame the teachers for something.

case of league tables, letting everybody know about it. However, in some junior schools testing is also used in order to "stream" pupils. By this I don't mean that they dip them in water if they get things wrong (although they might), I mean that they use testing as a way of grouping people of like ability together, so that the bright pupils work with the bright pupils, the not-so-bright work with the not-so-bright, and the really thick ones work with the teacher.[1]

This test might be a formal sit-down sort of test, or it might be based on classroom work. Either way you get lumped together with children of the same ability. But what if you're just a bit of a slow starter? You know, somebody who's actually more on the ball than the teachers at first realize? Maybe you're a bit shy or you've missed a lot of school due to illness or you keep falling asleep (it happens to lots of us). Well, hopefully this gets spotted and you get moved to the correct group. If not, you carry on working in the wrong group.

Some schools don't stream pupils. They teach in what's called "mixed ability" groups. The theory here is

1: Who's probably even thicker than *they* are!

that the bright pupils will help the not-so-bright, and the lazy ones will get away with it.

COR! THANKS FOR HELPING ME WITH THE SCIENCE PROJECT, BRIGHT KIDS!

SHUT UP AND LIGHT THE BLUE TOUCH PAPER

Or something. But the point is that all this is achieved by testing of some sort, because (as you begin to realize about this time) schools are very keen on testing of *any* sort. They'd use it for everything if they could – even cleaning the floor.

At junior school you start to notice a different approach to exams and testing. No longer do the teachers sneak around attempting to assess you without your knowing about it; you don't spend a week feeling totally confused, only to discover later that you've been doing SATs. No! At juniors they not only admit that they're testing you, they shout it from the rooftops. Now, on the one hand this is easier to handle because you know what's going on, but on the other it's far more stressful because it means that suddenly you have to prepare for tests. You have to work, because everybody knows about it and so you'll soon get caught out if you don't.

Everyone around you becomes obsessed with the tests. Not just the "swotty" kids – everyone. The teachers even send notes home to your parents warning them that you've got a test. The notes usually say something along the lines of "Could you make sure that your child gets to bed at a reasonable time (i.e. some time before three in the morning) as he/she has a test tomorrow?" What the note is actually saying is that your parents should help you prepare for the test. Really? Has your teacher ever *met* your parents?

Hard to believe, I know, but there *are* parents who take that amount of interest in their children. Others just don't bother.

So what sort of tests do you get in junior school? Well, of course there's more of those lovely SATs. They were such a big hit when you were seven (or at least they caused several parents to hit teachers) that it was decided that they should be repeated at 11[1]. Unlikely though it may sound, SATs are quite useful at junior school. For one thing they can help sort out what secondary school you go to.

1: And again at secondary school at 14. Aren't you lucky!

Any school that is considered to be the best in the area can really call the shots. And what happens is that a lot of these schools devise their own entrance exam in order to ensure that they only get the cream of the available pupils. It's a *formal* examination, and as such it's probably the first one of its kind that you will have encountered – if you take it, that is.[1] What do I mean by formal? Well, it usually takes place in the school hall, which annoys the dinner ladies and makes them clatter about even more than usual. Also, during the actual exam there'll not only be teachers present, but there's usually an Outside Examiner as well.[2] By this I don't mean that he or she will be outside with their nose pressed against the window or watching the whole thing on closed-circuit television. I mean that this examiner might be a teacher from another school (even the school you're hoping to be selected for), a qualified school inspector, or somebody who's wandered in off the street by accident. There's often no way of knowing.

A QUALIFIED SCHOOL INSPECTOR

SOMEONE WHO'S WANDERED IN OFF THE STREET

You and all your mates who are also taking the test will be sitting in rows, far enough apart to make whispering and note-passing virtually impossible. Of course some of your mates might not be there. They might have had the "bright idea" of going sick for the

1: Most entrance exams will be very similar, although some may take place at the school of your choice, giving you the added stress of having to get there on the bus!
2: See Outside Examiner in the A–Z section for more details.

34

day. I say "bright idea", but actually it's a really dim idea because they'll only make you take the test another day, or worse still make you go to some really hideous school that nobody, not even a teacher, is prepared to set foot in. In fact, selection tests throw up (sometimes literally) quite a number of problems for the examinee – that's you. These problems are:

1) How well do I want to do? Because if I do too badly I'll get sent to some awful place that's actually been condemned but nobody has got the nerve to go in there and tell anybody. But if I do too well I might get sent to some school that makes me work really, really hard in the mistaken belief that I actually enjoy school work.

2) How well will I be able to do? Because this is no normal school situation where, if you don't know the answer to something, you can ask somebody or just make something up.[1] You also have no idea what sort of questions they're going to ask. Oh yes, your teacher may have given you a few hints, but you can be pretty sure

1: After all, the teacher's never going to look at it, are they?

that whatever your teacher tells you is bound to be wrong. After all she was wrong about Preston being the capital of China, wasn't she?[1]

3) How well do my parents want me to do? And this is of course a complete minefield. Yes, they may *say* that they want you to go to the local Grammar, but when they get the list of stuff they have to provide – uniform, equipment, books and so on – you'll soon hear them saying things like: "D'you know, I think it's a pity that kids aren't sent out to work as soon as they get their own teeth."

Then of course there's all the other considerations such as what school are your mates going to get into? Which school has the best football/netball team? Which one goes on the most trips, has the dishiest teachers, etc.? Yes, the entrance exam is only a part of the problem of secondary selection, but it is the worst part. And (as I said earlier) it's your first real taste of proper exams – exams that will continue not only for the rest of your school life but your natural life too. It's when you first get into a testing or examination experience such as this that you start to realize several basic ground rules:

1) Teachers don't help.

2) Strong underwear doesn't help.

3) You're on your own.

Of course you've been on your own before, lots of times. "Lost and Alone" could be your middle name, if it wasn't Roger or Melanie.[2] But then that's the price we pay for being young. We're expected to know things and expected to do things without any real help. And if grown-ups aren't criticizing us for not knowing stuff, then they're giving us impossible tests just to try to prove that we're not as smart as they are.[3] And we really get to learn the truth of this when we reach...

1: Even though you didn't realize it for some years.
2: Or something different.
3: See also the Cycling Proficiency Test.

Big school

Another name for secondary school. This nickname derives from the fact that all secondary schools are much bigger than their primary counterparts, apart from the ones that are smaller, of course. But once you settle into Big School, get used to the bullying, the dinners and the fact that it takes two years to find your classroom, you quickly realize a big truth – *secondary school is a testing environment.*

Life soon becomes one long test with bits of lessons and lunch crammed in between. And the longer you stay there, the worse it gets. Oh yes, you do get the occasional hour off for good behaviour – this is called "detention" – but apart from that there's a test round every corner.

You're in the middle of a French lesson, when suddenly the teacher announces that she's going to test your knowledge of French verbs. Why? What good is that to anybody? After all, if you go to France and can't speak the language, understanding how verbs are declined isn't going to be a lot of use, is it? Shouting and waving your arms would probably help you get along better. Then there's exercise. You get your kit on for a few hours in the gym, and what happens? The PE teacher suddenly decides to have an impromptu test to see who looks funniest trying to get over the vaulting horse. In English you get spelling, in Maths you get sums and in Science you get "Who can blow everyone else up the quickest?" And where is it all leading? To your GCSEs!

GCSE stands for General Certificate of Secondary Education, and as such it's the culmination of all the testing that you've ever done in school. And if you enjoy GCSEs, which most people don't, you can stay in school and do a harder version – "A" level GCSEs.[1] But more of those later.

GCSEs start to rear their ugly head(s) as you reach Year 9, when you'll be expected to choose which subjects you want to be tested on in Year 11.

1: Known in Scotland as "Highers".

"That's two years from now! How can I be expected to know what I'll fancy in two years' time?"

This is probably what you'll feel like saying and you'd be right. Two years *is* a long time – in fact for a two-year-old it's a lifetime. But these are grown-ups we're dealing with. They don't understand such logic.

There are certain questions you can ask yourself to help you decide which options to go for. For instance:

1) What am I interested in? Logic says that if you're interested in something you'll make an effort to be good at it. Of course in practice this is rarely the case, but it does provide a good starting point. Decide what you're interested in and select these subjects for study to GCSE level. But think carefully. Not all subjects are available for examination. As a simple rule of thumb, if you pick stuff like English, Maths and Geography you're on a safe bet, but if you pick stuff like rollerblading, hanging about the Arndale Centre and cheeking your brother, you might find that these exams aren't available (yet).[1]

2) What am I good at? As we've just established this may not be something that you enjoy, but obviously you're going to score higher marks doing a subject that you're good at than you will doing something you haven't the first idea about.

3) What do my teachers think? Very little, usually, but given a bit of encouragement (and a lot of cash) they may be persuaded to advise you on your GCSE options.

1: Incidentally if you pick your nose, you'll be unlikely to be able to get anyone to examine it.

4) What do my parents think? For a slightly less stressful life it's a good idea not to discuss your exam options with your parents. Unfortunately parents don't see it like this. They insist on being involved in their child's education, even though they can't remember their child's name. This can cause more problems than it solves because often parents want you to take the subjects they took, even though you clearly hate them.

YOU SHOULD STUDY WOODWORK SON – JUST LIKE I DID!

What they don't tell you is that they hated them too, and they don't see why they should be the only ones to suffer.

There are of course ways to help you deal with the above, so that you can get on with selecting your options. Try this simple test:

1) Which lessons do I fall asleep in? This should tell you which ones you hate and which ones you're no good at. On the other hand it might just tell you that you love that particular subject so much that you're working far too hard at it, and that's why you're falling asleep.

2) Which lessons do my teachers fall asleep in? This should tell you which subjects you're unlikely to get the necessary help with – help you'll almost certainly need if you're going to get a GCSE in them. On the other hand

it might just tell you that your teacher never gets to bed early enough.

3) Do my parents fall asleep when I start asking them which subjects I should do? This should tell you whether or not your parents are interested in your future. On the other hand it might just tell you that it was a really bad idea to try and have a serious discussion about your future at four in the morning.

You see none of this is easy and this is why it's so stressful. The only thing you can be absolutely sure about is that at some point you are going to have to make some decisions about what options you take. Even if you don't you're still going to get tested on them. That is as certain as night follows day. So how do you prepare yourself for the inevitable? Read on.

Ready, Steady, Test!

There are several ways that you can prepare for exams. The following advice applies not only to GCSEs but to any type of formal exam that might get thrown at you at some point in your life, and therefore it's best to be fully prepared. So let's get our heads down and study the options.

There are a number of books offering advice on how to pass exams. One of the first things they advise is setting yourself a timetable for study. Good idea. At least it is if you know *what* to study in the first place! Because as we've already established, examiners are entitled to ask you anything they like, as long as it has a vague connection with the subject. For instance any questions in Maths must have a bit of a sum in them somewhere, though whether you'll be able to spot it is another matter.

...AND DO YOU HAVE ANY 'HOW TO STUDY' BOOKS ABOUT HOW TO STUDY 'HOW TO STUDY' BOOKS?

But we'll deal with the actual exam later. At the moment we need to imagine that the exam is about six months away. So what should you be doing? Panicking maybe, especially if you've done no work up to now.

Let's assume that you've done a bit. After all, it's almost impossible to go to school every day without doing any work at all, even if you only do it by accident. Let's assume that you've done enough work to be able to know which options you have most chance of passing – or least chance of failing. How then do you prepare for the Big Day? You need a plan. Here's one:

Study

You do need to study, I suppose. Partly to catch up on the stuff you missed, slept through, or otherwise managed to avoid, and partly to make sure that you understand it. Let's face it, just because a teacher tells you something it doesn't necessarily mean that it's going to make any sense to you. In fact the chances of understanding anything a teacher says are pretty slim. This is another reason why you need to study. But how? Like this:

1) Work out a timetable of study, in addition to the stuff you're doing at school. Obviously if you've got free study periods then you can build these into your timetable as well.

2) Make sure you spread all the subjects you're studying evenly across your timetable. It's also quite a good idea to vary the subject order from week to week, so that you don't get bored. You'll get bored anyway, but this might help to reduce it.

3) If there's a subject that you're less confident about then allow more time on your study timetable for this one. Obviously if you're no good at *anything* this could be a bit tricky.

4) Set yourself achievable goals on your timetable. It's pointless scheduling the study of the entire 18th century for one afternoon, for example – particularly if you're not doing GCSE History.

5) Build break and rest periods into your timetable – it's just as important to relax as it is to study.

To illustrate the points above I have prepared a typical timetable. Feel free to adopt it as your own, changing the subjects to suit your chosen options.

	8AM–12	12 — 4PM	4PM – 10PM	10PM– 8AM
MON	Geog	Maths	Physics	
TUE	French	Biology		
WED	Physics		English	S
THUR	English	Geog	History	L
FRI	French	Biology	Maths	E
SAT	English	History		E
SUN	History			P

As you can see, I've taken the "achievable goals" bit very seriously indeed.

You might also find it helpful to get a friend to study with. It's a good idea *not* to choose that totally gorgeous person from 3b, partly because they won't be studying for GSCEs yet, and partly because if they're around, neither will you. The ideal person to help you study is somebody very, very intelligent who knows all the answers. That way you don't have to look so many things up. If you can arrange to pick somebody who also has the power to turn themselves into harmless-looking everyday objects such as fountain pens, then you have the added advantage of being able to smuggle them into the exam without raising suspicion. After all, examiners are more interested in catching people talking, eating, passing notes or killing and stuffing wildebeest than stopping them talking to their pens. In fact most examination boards accept that talking to your pen is a common side-effect of examination stress.

Eating for two GCSEs

The right food is essential to examination success. Now obviously I'm not talking about eating during the exam – we've already established that that won't be allowed.[1] I'm referring to a healthy diet. As anyone with even a vague understanding of nutrition will tell you, the right diet helps you to concentrate, gives you energy, and stops you getting spots. Spots can really slow you down in an exam situation, especially if they keep exploding all over your exam paper.

Of course there's no need to deny yourself all your favourite things. This is an exam you're entering, not a monastery. For instance cutting your chocolate bar intake by half should be sufficient, unless of course that means cutting it from 20 bars a day to ten. And you can allow yourself the occasional bag of crisps, as long as "occasional" doesn't mean every three minutes. Fish is good. Fish is "brain food" which is really surprising because fish are universally stupid, even the really intelligent ones. They just swim around calling each other *Bob* all day. But a nice big plate of fish – with chips, mushy peas and a couple of pickled gherkins – is bound to set you off on the right track. To where I'm not sure, but still, here are a couple more eating ideas that should ensure a healthy intake of essential vitamins whilst making sure that you keep your sugar level up.

SYRUP-COATED CARROT (WITH HUNDREDS AND THOUSANDS)

Ingredients:
One large carrot (20cm)
One jar of syrup
500g of hundreds and thousands

PTO→

1: It's quite possible that one day GCSE "Eating as Much as Possible Without Exploding" will be introduced. If that has happened by the time you read this book, please accept my apologies.

Method:
Peel and wash carrot. Pour entire contents of jar of syrup over carrot, placing mouth below carrot to catch any drips. Roll carrot in "hundreds and thousands" Eat. Say "Never again!" Throw up.
(I appreciate that there's quite a bit of effort involved in this recipe, but it'll be worth it)

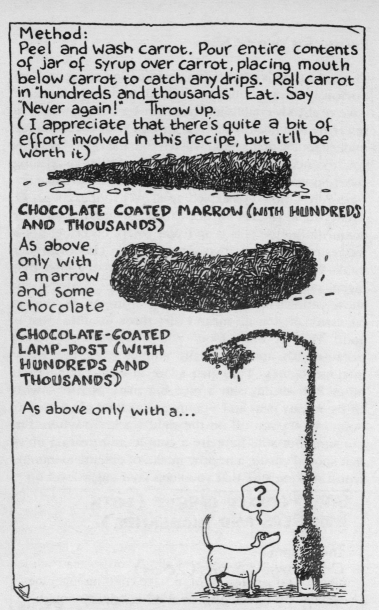

CHOCOLATE COATED MARROW (WITH HUNDREDS AND THOUSANDS)

As above, only with a marrow and some chocolate

CHOCOLATE-COATED LAMP-POST (WITH HUNDREDS AND THOUSANDS)

As above only with a...

Yes, OK, maybe a lamp-post is going too far. But the message is clear: eat the right food.

You can add food breaks to your weekly study plan. The revised plan would now look something like this:

	8AM 8.30	8.30 11	11 11.15	11.15 12.00	12.00 12.30	12.30 3.45	3.45 4.00	4.00 7.30	7.30 8.30	8.30 10.00	10.00PM 8.AM
MON		Geog		Geog		Hist		Hist		Hist	
TUE		Fr		Fr		Biol		Biol		Biol	
WED	B	Phys	E	Plays	D	Eng	A	Eng		Eng	S
THUR	R	Eng	L	Eng	I	Eng	T	Geog	T	Geog	L
FRI	E	Fr	E	Fr	N	Fr	A	Maths	E	Maths	E
SAT	A	Hist	V	Hist	N	Hist	S	Maths	A		E
SUN	K	Fr	E	Fr	E	Fr	N	Maths			P

(vertical column labels: BREAKFAST, ELEVENSES, DINNER, A TASTY SNACK, TEA, SLEEP)

Fighting fit

I'm sure that you're bright enough to realize that there's absolutely no point in eating the right food unless you also take some exercise. The best idea is to try and build exercise into your studying plan. That way it becomes a part of your daily routine. Make sure that your study allows for a certain amount of exercise. Don't, for instance, study in bed. By not doing so you build a little gentle walking into your study routine, even if it is only crossing the room to your desk. Avoid any kind of labour-saving devices, such as paying your kid brother to turn the pages of your textbook for you. Obviously it makes sense to try and structure your exercise routine so that it doesn't stop you studying. Jogging on a running machine (or even running on a jogging machine), for instance, would allow you to read while running. Of course not all of us have running machines. I haven't got any. But anyone who is bright enough to take GCSEs should be able to invent a simple running device. Here's a suggestion:

This is a simple and inexpensive idea: most of us have got skates or rollerblades (even my granny), so by tying yourself to a strong doorknob with a piece of rope you should be able to run and read at the same time. Incidentally, the fan provides fresh air, which is absolutely essential for keeping your brain sharp.

If you prefer to read outdoors, then the following suggestion might suit you better:

This is slightly more dangerous, as the risk of serious injury to yourself, your dog or your book is very real. You also can't rely on the dog to have a good knowledge of the local area,[1] which is why I've provided him with a street map.

Of course this may all be a bit low-tech for you. After all, we do live in the age of the microchip. You can even

1: Unless he's got GCSE Orienteering.

get micro-fish as well, apparently. So why not put all the information you want to study on to a tape and pop it in your personal stereo? A word of warning here: make sure that you've got a suitable personal stereo.

Running may not be your idea of exercise. It certainly isn't mine. In which case you need to find something else. Press-ups and sit-ups are a good idea.

These are a good physical challenge for the body and also let you carry on studying, as long as you put the book in the right place.

The only problem with this method of study, as far as I can see, is that you'll only be able to read your text-book as it gets close to your face. You also might find yourself reading the same sentence over and over again, particularly when fatigue sets in.

Not all forms of exercise are suited to study. Aerobics, for instance, is probably not the ideal exercise to attempt while revising.

Make sure that you also plot your exercise regime into your study schedule. It should now look something like this:

	7 AM 8 AM	8-8.30	8.30 11.00	11-11.15	11.15 12	12-12.30	12.30 3.45	3.45 4.00	4-4.30	4.30 7.30	7.30 8.30	8.30 10.00	10.00 7 AM
MON			Geog		Geog		Math			Math		Phys	
TUE			Fr		Fr		Bio			Biol		Biol	
WED	JOG 10 MILES	BREAKFAST	Phys	ELEVENSES	Phys	DINNER	Eng	SNACK	500 PRESS-UPS	Eng	TEA	Eng	SLEEP
THUR			Eng		Eng		Eng			Geog		Geog	
FRI			Fr		Fr		Fr			Maths		Maths	
SAT			Eng		Eng		Eng			Maths		Maths	
SUN			Hist		Hist		Hist			Fr		Fr	

Leisure and pleasure

Leisure is essential if you're going to get through your study schedule. Leisure activities play a vital part in preparing you for the trauma of exams. TV, for instance, is a very good way of unwinding after a hard study period. But you have to plan ahead. It's no good wasting valuable study time by staring at the TV guide wondering what to watch. A good way to organize yourself is to take the TV guide to the loo or into the bath with you and use that time to plan your day's viewing. A word of warning here: make sure you don't get the TV guide submerged in the bath water, otherwise you'll have to use a snorkel to read it. Also select only the programmes you want to watch, and write the times on to your plan carefully so that you don't go over time. You have to be very strict with yourself. The minute the programme finishes switch off the set and go back to your room to study. If you have a TV in your room it's best not to use that one, or you might be tempted to leave it on. If you plot your viewing time carefully your schedule should now look something like this:

	7.AM 8.AM	8- 8.30	8.30 11	11 11.15	11.15 12	12- 12.30	12.30 1.30	1.30 4.15	4.15 5	5 5.30	5.30 8.30	8.30 9.30	9.30 10.00	10.30 12	12 1AM
MON	JOG 10 MILES	BREAKFAST	Geo	ELEVENSES	Geo	DINNER	T.V.	Med,	SNACK	PRESS-UPS	Med,	TEA	T.V.	Maths	SLEEP
TUE			Fr.		Fr			Bio			Bio			Bio	
WED			Eng		Eng			Hist			Hist			Maths	
THUR			Bio		Bio			Phys			Phys			Fr.	
FRI			Phys		Phys			Eng			Eng			Maths	
SAT			Hist		Hist			Bio			Bio			Eng	
SUN			Fr		Fr			Eng			Fr			Fr	

An exam of two halves

Sport is also important to your overall well-being during the run-up to an exam, assuming that you play one.[1] If you don't this is probably the ideal time to take one up. Sport is a very good way of getting rid of pent-up tension, and believe me, studying for exams is about the quickest way to get tense, if only because your parents keep saying things like, "Have you done any studying today?" Don't they realize that the time you waste

1: A sport that is – not an exam. You can't play exams, but then you knew that – didn't you?

saying, "Er … no", could be better spent studying? Of course they don't! They're grown-ups after all, and as such they're just another source of stress. Stress that can be disastrous to exam success, but fortunately can also be greatly relieved by playing a sport.

Even sport can be combined with study, in subtle and clever ways. Football, for instance, could be combined with studying for a Maths GCSE. How? I'll tell you. But first answer this question: What is the single greatest thing that prevents most of us ordinary mortals becoming mathematical geniuses? (Don't say: "The fact that maths is boring", even if you're right.) The greatest stumbling block to mathematical success is mathematical formulas – or formulae as they should more rightly be called. Did you know that? No? Well, no wonder you're no good at it.[1] But they are. And the main thing about mathematical formulae is that they are impossible to remember. They're designed that way. Let's face it, if they were easy to remember then most of the mystery about maths would disappear overnight. Without complex and seemingly pointless formulae maths would just be *adding up*.[2] But how do you remember this stuff while enjoying the contact sport camaraderies of a game of football? Easy! You write the formulae all over the ball! That way, as you dribble the ball along you can be checking out the formulae on the way. Or if you're a goalie you can check it out as you pick the ball out of the back of the net. Obviously you need to be careful not to put too much spin on the ball, otherwise you're likely to get the formulae muddled together as they flash past you in a blur.

Some of you may be saying, "But I don't play a lot of football." Well, the same principle could be applied to netball or basketball. It might be less effective during a

---

1: If you didn't know that the plural of *formula* is *formulae* either then you're probably not much good at English either. Never mind – there are other things in life. Like juggling.
2: Actually it *is* just adding up.

game of cricket, rounders, tennis or any game that involves a smaller ball. Badminton would probably be a non-starter as you would only really be able to write stuff on the knobbly end bit of the shuttlecock. Squash would not be a good idea for a number of reasons: not only is the ball too small to get many formulae on to its surface, but the speed it travels would make any attempts to read it extremely dangerous.

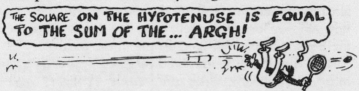

This same method could be used for scientific data, as long as it was only something like the chemical formula for titanium. Quotations from Shakespeare for use in studying his plays might be a waste of time, although you could write them on the sight-screen if you're playing cricket.

It's quite possible that many of you feel that combining sport and revision is a bit of a waste of both things – and you could be right. In which case make sure you schedule enough time on your study timetable to allow for a decent session of sport. Your schedule should now look something like this:

	7AM–8AM	8–8.30	8.30–11	11–11.15	11.15–12	12–12.30	12.30–1.30	1.30–3.30	3.30–6	6–6.15	6.15–6.45	6.45–9	9–10	10–11	11–12	2AM–7AM
MON	JOG	BREAKFAST	Geo	ELEVENSES	Geo	DINNER	T.V.	SPORT	M	SNACK	PRESS-UPS	M	TEA	T.V.	Ph	SLEEP
TUE	JOG	BREAKFAST	Fr	ELEVENSES	Fr	DINNER	T.V.	SPORT	Ph	SNACK	PRESS-UPS	Bio	TEA	T.V.	Bio	SLEEP
WED	JOG	BREAKFAST	Eng	ELEVENSES	Eng	DINNER	T.V.	SPORT	Fr	SNACK	PRESS-UPS	Fr	TEA	T.V.	Ma	SLEEP
THUR	JOG	BREAKFAST	Bio	ELEVENSES	Bio	DINNER	T.V.	SPORT	Pl	SNACK	PRESS-UPS	Pl	TEA	T.V.	Fr	SLEEP
FRI	JOG	BREAKFAST	Phys	ELEVENSES	Phys	DINNER	T.V.	SPORT	Eng	SNACK	PRESS-UPS	Eng	TEA	T.V.	Eng	SLEEP
SAT	JOG	BREAKFAST	Hist	ELEVENSES	Hist	DINNER	T.V.	SPORT	Pl	SNACK	PRESS-UPS	Pl	TEA	T.V.	M	SLEEP
SUN	JOG	BREAKFAST	Eng	ELEVENSES	Eng	DINNER	T.V.	SPORT	Geo	SNACK	PRESS-UPS	Geo	TEA	T.V.	E	SLEEP

Relax, why don't you

Tension is the second greatest cause of exam failure. Not turning up is the first. So, assuming that you intend to turn up, how do you make sure that you're relaxed enough to attempt the exam paper? Well, for a start it's not just a case of making sure that you're relaxed on the day. That would be almost impossible, if you haven't already trained yourself in relaxation techniques. But how do you do this? Well, here are a few suggested methods that have worked for me in the past:

1) **The quick method.** Stand in front of a mirror. Make sure that you've got your clothes on because suddenly starting to laugh can really spoil this technique. Look yourself squarely in the eyes.[1] (Eye-contact is absolutely essential to the success of the technique.) Having got your own attention, say firmly: "If you don't relax I'm

going to hit you over the head with this large piece of wood." The only problem with this method is that you have to be prepared to carry the threat through. If you aren't, then how can you possibly expect to be able to convince yourself that you are? And if you aren't convinced that the threat is real then it's not a threat, is it? The other unfortunate by-product of this method is that, if you do carry the threat through, you could be unconscious for the entire duration of the exam – but at least you'd be relaxed.

2) **The short sharp shock.** You may feel that the above method is a short sharp shock, but I can assure you that it isn't when compared to this method. Again

1: If you haven't got square eyes then look yourself *roundly* in the eyes.

it involves looking yourself in the eye via a mirror. Again, having got your attention, you simply say to yourelf: "You know, if you don't relax immediately *you're going to fail this exam*!" The best method of delivering this bit of sound advice is to start in a calm and reasonable fashion, rising to a screaming frenzy

towards the end. If you can manage to foam at the mouth this adds credibility to the statement and certainly ought to convince you that you mean business. The obvious advantage this has over the other method is that there is little or no risk of brain damage brought about by being whacked on the head with a lump of wood. Extensive research has shown that brain damage can have a negative effect on exam success.

3) **The gentle touch.** This method – if started early enough in your study schedule – may prove the safest bet. It doesn't involve any unpleasantly loud shouting or threats with bits of wood. However, it is a much slower process, and can take months to develop.

Lie on a bed in a darkened room, preferably in your own house. Lying on a bed in a darkened room in a complete stranger's house can be distressing for both you and the stranger, particularly if they live alone. So choose your own room. Having got yourself into a lying position (*see diagram if you're not*

sure what that is), close your eyes. Then focus on each part of your body in turn, while saying: "Toes … you are relaxed. Feet … you are relaxed. Legs … you are relaxed. Knees … you are relaxed. Thighs … you are relaxed. Er…" Perhaps you don't have to worry about relaxing *every* part of your body, but you get the general idea. Work your way up your body until you reach your brain – which you'll probably find in your head. When you reach this point simply say: "Relax … relax … you are feeling relaxed … you are fee…" Sorry! I nodded off there for a second. But then I've been using this sophisticated and complex relaxation method for years. You may find that you can't completely relax your body the very first time you try this method, but it's worth persevering.

How will you know that you've achieved the necessary level of relaxation? Well, there is a simple test you can try in order to determine this. All you need is an old pair of trousers and a box of matches. Put the trousers on and set fire to them. If you can remain relaxed while they blaze, then you're definitely ready to be examined![1]

You'll almost certainly need to build these relaxation periods into your study schedule, which should now be looking something like this:

	6AM 7AM	7-8 8-30	8- 8:30	8:30 11	11- 11:15	11:15 12	12 12:30	12:30 1:30	1:30 3:30	3:30 9:30	3:30 6:30	6:30 6:45	6:45 2:15	7:15 10	10 11	11 12	12:3 3	3-6
MON				Geo		Geog					M			M			Phy	
TUE				Fr		Fr					Bio			Bio			Bio	
WED	R E L A X	J O G	B R E A K F A S T	Eng	E L E V E N S E S	Eng	D I N N E R	T.V.	S P O R T	R E L A X	Fr	S N A C K	P R E S S - U P S	Fr	T E A	T.V.	Maths	S L E E P
THUR				Eng		Eng					Fr			Phy				
FRI				Maths		Maths					Eng			Eng			Eng	
SAT				Phys		Phys					Chem			Geo			Chem	
SUN				Hist		Hist								News			Maths	

1: Examined and committed! Wearing blazing trousers is probably about the silliest thing you can do, especially just before an exam. Wearing them *during* the exam could get you disqualified. It would certainly make it hard to concentrate.

56

A helping hand

One of the things about exams that many people over-look is the amount of writing you're going to be doing, particularly with *written* exams. If you are sitting a written exam and you manage to go the whole length of the exam without writing a single word, it's probably safe to say that you won't gain an "A" grade – or any grade at all, probably. But if you do the exam properly, then the chances are that you'll be doing so much writing you'll barely have time to read the exam paper.

Now you can probably imagine the kind of strain this is going to put on your writing hand. After all, just writing to your granny to say: "Hi Gran thanks for the jumper" gives you chronic hand-ache, and that hasn't even got any punctuation in it. So how do you deal with this problem? There are a number of methods but getting someone to do the writing for you isn't one of them. Examiners are usually quite sharp people and they tend to spot anyone who is using a "ghost" writer, even if the examinee has got them hidden under their school blazer.

The only sensible way to avoid "writer's cramp", as it is not surprisingly called, is to exercise your hand muscles. How? Probably the simplest and cheapest method is to squeeze a rubber ball. Buy, borrow or find a small rubber ball and keep clenching and unclenching it in your fist. This should build up the muscles in your hand and fingers. But be careful not to overdo it.

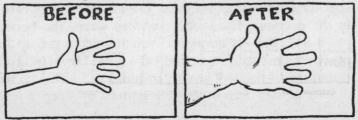

The great thing about this method is that it can be done at any time, even when you're fully occupied with other activities, except maybe going to the loo. However, if you want to make it a separate activity, build it into your schedule, which will then start to look not a million miles different from this one:

	6AM 7	7-8	8-9	9-9:30	9:30-12	12-12:45	12:45-3	3-3:50	3:50-4:30	6:30-5:30	5:30-7:30	7:30-8:50	8:30-11:30	11:30-11:45	11:45-12	12-3AM	3-4	4-4:30	9:30-5	5AM 6AM
MON	RELAX	JOG	HAND EXERCISE	BREAKFAST	ELEVENSES	DINNER	T.V.	HAND EXERCISES	SPORT	RELAX	SNACK	PRESS-UPS	TEA	T.V.	HAND EXERCISES					
TUE																				
WED																				
THUR																				
FRI																				
SAT																				
SUN																				

The ravelled sleeve of time

It was Shakespeare who said that "Sleep kits up the ravelled sleeve of time." Unfortunately he never explained what it meant, which is a great pity because it's exactly the sort of thing you're likely to get asked in an exam. I mention it because sleep is essential to exam success.

Even a few hours of good sound sleep can make all the difference between a pass and a fail, especially if you do the sleeping during an exam. The message is "Go to bed!" Not now! Come back! I mean at night.

On the night before an exam go to bed as soon as you start feeling the least bit tired, even if this is very early in the evening. The longer you can sleep, the better you'll feel. But set an alarm. You'll need to get up in plenty of time to shower and eat a good breakfast. You can't think if you feel grubby or hungry.

Start getting into a sensible pattern of sleep a few

58

weeks before the exam. It's no good staying out all night for weeks and then suddenly having an early night just before the actual test. Tiredness creeps up on you like a caretaker's dog. Decide what sort of sleep pattern will suit you and build it into your timetable, the final version of which should not look like this:

	6AM-7	7-8	8-9	9-9.30	9.30-12	12-12.30	12.30-3	3-3.30	3.30-4.30	4.30-5.30	5.30-7.30	7.30-8.30	8.30-11.30	11.30-11.45	11.45-12	12-3AM	3AM-4	4-5	5-6	6AM-9AM
MON	RELAX	JOG	HAND EXERCISE	BREAKFAST	ELEVENSES	DINNER	T.V.	HAND EXERCISES	SPORT	RELAX	SNACK	PRESS-UPS	TEA	T.V.	HAND EXERCISES	SLEEP				
TUE																				
WED																				
THUR																				
FRI																				
SAT																				
SUN	SLEEP																			

Ah. Oh dear! Perhaps we need a rethink. I know! Let's knock the revision on the head.

	7-8AM	8-9	9-9.30	9.30-10	10-11	11-11.30	11.30-12.30	12.30-1.30	1.30-2	2-3	3-3.30	3.30-5.30	5.30-6	6-7	7-10	10PM-7AM
MON	RELAX	JOG	HAND EXERCISE	BREAKFAST	SLEEP	ELEVENSES	SPORT	DINNER	HAND EXERCISES	RELAX	SNACK	T.V.	PRESS-UPS	TEA	MORE T.V.	SLEEP
TUE																
WED																
THUR																
FRI																
SAT																
SUN																

There is a school of thought that claims that there's no point in revising because you either know stuff or you don't. I wish I'd gone to that school! In a way this argument is a perfectly good one. It's true that you do either know something or you don't. Whether or not

59

you'll *remember* it when you get into the exam is another matter! That's why you need to revise – to make sure that you *do* remember stuff. Because once you get into the exam room – as I said earlier – *you are on your own*!

Halls of panic

Let's jump forward now to the day of the exam. You've done all your preparation (sort of), you've kept yourself fit (sort of), and now you're ready for whatever gets thrown at you (er…). Your mum got you up early, you've showered (or washed or just looked at the tap), you've had a good breakfast and you're as ready as you'll ever be. Yes – you're probably right to panic! No you're not! You've got to think positive.

Yes! That's it! Think positive! Keep telling yourself that you can do it!

Of course it doesn't help when your parents keep saying things like, "You can only do your best." What does that mean? And anyway it's not true! You can do your *worst*! Quite easily! In fact you probably will! Although … why should you? After all, what is this? Just a stupid exam set by some grown-ups you've never met in an attempt to try and prove that you're not as clever as you think you are. Why are they bothering? What does it matter to them? And besides, they're wrong! You *are* as clever as you think you are. It's just that you don't happen to *think* that you're very clever, that's all. The problem with exams is that they're surrounded by such mystique, such fuss and such nonsense, it's hard to remember what they're all about. So let's get one thing straight: *Exams are a way of discovering how much you know about things that you've already been taught*. And if you haven't been taught them, that's hardly your fault, is it? But since exams are set by the same sort of people who determine the National Curriculum, then it stands to reason that you're not going to be asked about things you've never heard of.

The truth is, of course, that it's not the *content* of the exams that's so scary, it's the *thought* of them, and all the pressure that surrounds them. You worry about the expectations that parents have of you – expectations that frankly they should keep to themselves. What good is it going to do you if they tell you how disappointed they'll be if you do badly in an exam? Who is this exam for anyway, them or you? Why do you need to know beforehand that you'll be letting your teacher down if you don't do as well as they think you should? So what if you don't? They'll get over it. And if they don't get over it, what are they going to do? Tell you off? Keep you in? Throw themselves off the science block roof?

Unfortunately you take all this baggage into the room with you, even through the rules expressly state that you must not bring any additional stuff into the exam room, apart from things like a pen to write with and a hanky to cry into.

So leave the baggage outside, and follow me.

Examining the exams

The first thing that strikes you when you enter an exam room is the icy chill of the examiner's breath. No, that's not true! The first thing is usually how different the school hall looks without bits of food stuck all over the floor. Old Mr Volestrangler, the caretaker, has really excelled himself. But then he's always been a great believer in the value of education. Pity he left school when he was five really, otherwise he might have some understanding of what you're going through.

So what *are* you going through? Well, right now you're in the hall, waiting to be totally confused (or so you believe) by the exam paper that is being placed on every desk in the room. All this under the watchful and eagle eye of a teacher, the Head, or an Outside Examiner.[1] One thing you can be certain of is that supervising an exam brings out the worst in a person, though if you were brave enough to ask them, they would tell you that they are just doing their job, which is:

1) To make sure that everyone who has to have one, gets an exam paper. After extensive research it was realized that there was a link between exam success and receiving an exam paper in the first place. From a sample of 100 assorted pupils, the research showed that those pupils who were given an exam paper did measurably better than those who weren't. As a result, greater care is taken to make sure

1: I mentioned these earlier, remember? Do try and keep up – there might be a short test later!

that all examinees receive a paper before the exam starts.
2) To make sure that everyone understands the rules
governing the actual exam. These may range from "no
talking" right through to "no cheating", "no learning
aids" (textbooks, teachers etc.) and "no barbecues".
3) To make sure that everyone has everything they need
in order to complete any task set them during the exam.
This can range from a ruler and set-square for technical
drawing through to paints etc. for an Art exam.
Strangely enough, they draw a line at you taking a 166
MHz Pentium multi-media laptop PC into the exam with
you, which seems a bit short-sighted to me, considering
that this is the computer age, but still…
4) To make sure, through the duration of the exam, that
the various rules governing eating, talking, drinking or
line-dancing are observed.
5) To … er … that's it, really.

Not a tricky job, you might think, but certainly one that your average examiner takes very seriously. Just because you're staring around the room it doesn't mean that you're hoping to be able to catch a glimpse of Melvin Cardboard's answer paper reflected in a particularly shiny bit of the ceiling. The thought had probably not even crossed your mind although now that I've mentioned it, it's not a bad idea at all! DON'T EVEN THINK ABOUT IT! Your average examiner has got the eyes of a hawk. OK, so they're in a matchbox, and she only takes them out when she's on her own so that she can poke them with a cotton bud and hear them go "squish", but still.[1] The fact is that any breach of rules during an exam only prolongs the agony, because it can mean that you have to resit the exam on another day. If that happens you've got to go all the way through the study process again. Could you handle that? Me neither! Best to get your head down and "do your best", whatever that means!

What's all this then?

This is a not unreasonable first reaction when the examiner gives you that fateful instruction: *You may now turn over your papers*. She might also add: *You may now turn over your stomachs*, because even if you don't they're going to turn over by themselves anyway. This is when you start to regret my earlier advice to eat a decent breakfast. There's a law of examinations that says something like: "Whatever is written in an exam paper, you can be sure that it bears no resemblance to anything you've ever learnt." Or so it seems when you first turn the paper over. This is a natural reaction and not one that should send you running, screaming, for the door.

1: I told you that examiners were weird. Even Bill Oddie wouldn't do that and he's really keen on birds of prey.

Come back! There is a sensible, intelligent approach to any exam paper. So try to imagine for the sake of argument that you are both sensible and intelligent.

Have you done that?

Do you need more time?

OK, I'll settle for "quite tall".

But if you can manage it, the sensible and intelligent approach would be to start by reading the exam paper through carefully. This will take a few minutes at most, as long as it's written in English.

"But it's bound to be! Isn't it?" I hear you cry.

Not necessarily. You see, some examination boards prepare papers for other countries and you might get given one of these by mistake. If you are, then it's as well to mention it before the exam starts. If you don't then you can't be expected to be taken seriously if you bring it up after you've failed.

"I only failed because the paper was written in Swahili!"

You must admit that it has all the hallmarks of a limp excuse for not being very clever, doesn't it? Even though it's true. It's actually unlikely that the examination board are going to believe you anyway, because to do so would be to admit their mistake, and they aren't going to do that. Would you? So...

RULE 1

Read the exam paper carefully.

RULE 2

Read it carefully again, just in case you missed something. After all, you're bound to be nervous, no matter how good you got at the relaxation exercises. So read it again.

Do you understand it now?

OK, so which bits *don't* you understand?

Would it be easier to ask which bits you *do* understand?

OK, so which bits *do* you understand?

Most people understand that bit at the top of the exam paper that tells you that it's an exam in English (or Maths or whatever).

Oh, come on! You must understand some of it.

No?

Well, all I can say is that you've very lucky this isn't the *real thing*.

WHAT!?!?!

Oh, sorry! Didn't I tell you? These are just the *mocks*! That's not a proper examiner at all! It's Mr Cranberry, the trainspotter who comes in to teach Year 8 Advanced Worm-Farming! He's wearing a disguise! I thought you would have realized that! Oh dear! You really have got a bad case of exam panic, haven't you? The teacher *did* tell you that we were having a mock exam. You must have been away.

MR CRANBERRY

REAL EXAMINER

"Mock exam?" I can hear the confusion in your voice. Let me explain.

No, please – don't mock!

Mock exams are a chance for you to have a *dummy run* before you have to suffer the real thing. They're also a chance for teachers to mock your efforts, which is not surprisingly why they're called "mocks". The exam papers used for mocks are quite often old exam papers from previous years. The problem with that is that you can quite easily be lulled into a false sense of security by thinking that you might get the same questions again in your *actual* exam.

I know this sounds silly (at least I hope it does!) but you'd be amazed at the number of pupils (myself included) who actually think that examiners would give you the same questions. The logic goes something like this: "This is such a horrible question, that they're *bound* to give it to us in the real exam." That's fairly sound logic, because that's just the sort of thing that grown-ups (which is what examiners are) would do. They find something that they know you really hate and they keep giving it to you, like parsley sauce.

Unfortunately, although examiners are adults, they're also far more devious than that. They would argue,

"Yes! That is a really nasty question, but I'm sure we can come up with an even nastier one." In fact they make it their job to. Even if it means staying up late and working until their brains burst, they will find that impossible question and give it to you in an exam. So although the "mocks" are a good "dry run", don't think – just because you did well in them – that you can cruise through the real thing.

So why bother with mocks? Well, apart from giving you a chance to sit a formal exam, something you may have done very little of, they're also a way of ensuring that you're taking the right options. Because even though it would be a bit late to change, you could drop certain subjects that you're not too hot on so that you can concentrate on others that you are.

AS SOON AS YOU'VE FINISHED THIS TOAST RACK I THINK YOU SHOULD CONSIDER DROPPING METAL-WORK...

So let's assume that you've done your mocks, had a breakdown, been told off by your teacher, been shouted at by your parents, rethought your options and that somehow – amazingly – you're still in the game! Wow! If you've come this far you're doing well. But don't sit back. Instead sharpen your wits and your pencil, because now it's time to go for...

The real thing

The approach to the real exam is much the same as the "mocks". The rules will be much the same, except that the penalty for breaking them will be stronger: death for forgetting your pencil, detention for burning the school down, that sort of thing. This should not affect your approach to the exam paper; you should still read it carefully twice and then:

RULE 3

Make sure you understand the rules governing the paper. For instance, it may say, "*Answer any THREE of these questions*" and give you a choice of seven. In which case just answer three, like they tell you to. Don't even attempt all seven, because you won't get extra points for answering the lot. Neither will you get extra points for answering the same question three times.

RULE 4

Before you begin to tackle the questions, fill in any personal details required. For instance, you'll be asked for your name, which you must write in a special place on the exam paper. DON'T FORGET TO DO THIS! Your paper could be sent almost anywhere to be marked,[1] and if hasn't got your name on it they won't know it's yours.[2] You also get extra points for knowing your own name!

Sometimes you are asked for information such as *Date of birth* (the answer to this is whatever your birthday is. Don't put "Next Friday") and *Sex* (the answer to this is either "Boy" or "Girl". Don't put: "Don't know" or even "Yes please"). Don't take too long over this bit.

1: Even to a secure mental institution.
2: Which may turn out to be a good thing!

RULE 5

Check whether or not the paper allows you to answer the questions in any order. If it does, then make sure that it's obvious which question you're answering by marking it in the margin, or in a place provided. This is important because it might not be obvious from your answer which question you've attempted!

If, on the other hand, the paper says that you must answer the questions in the order in which they're written, you must do that. A couple of *don'ts* here:
1) Don't waste time if you're genuinely stuck on a question; move on to another one. And...
2) Don't try and do the questions out of order by leaving a big space for the question you're planning to come back to. It might not be big enough when you come back to answer the question.

RULE 6

Plan your answers carefully. Make notes if necessary. Examiners don't like a lot of crossings out, mainly because they'll waste precious time trying to read it, thinking it's just bad handwriting. Remember, the more you irritate the examiner marking your paper, the lower the mark you'll get.

RULE 7

Work out in advance how much time you're going to spend on each question and try to stick to it, otherwise you'll almost certainly run out of time. By this I don't mean work it out three weeks in advance, obviously! I mean look at the paper, decide which questions to answer, decide how long each one might take, add a bit, keep a bit of time back for checking things through, and go for it.

REMEMBER: You won't be asked anything that you haven't already been taught. Examiners are interested as much in how you approach answers as the answers themselves.

Unless of course they're wrong.

You see, that's the thing about exams – you are expected to get the answers right. Now, in the case of some subjects this is quite easy. Maths, for instance. If you were to reply "43" to the question *"What is 54 minus 11?"* that would be regarded as a correct answer by anybody's standards. But if you replied "Enid Blyton" to the same sum, you'd probably find that you were wrong.

However, some subjects aren't as black and white. In English Literature, for instance, you might be asked to express opinions. For example, you might be asked to *"Discuss the use of imagery in the writings of C.S. Lewis"*. What you won't know is whether or not your view is going to upset the person who marks your paper. There are proper ways of approaching things, and accepted views of particular subjects, which means that there's probably an accepted opinion about the use of imagery in the writings of … etc., etc. The thing is, do you know what that accepted opinion is? Do you care? Do you have the foggiest idea what I'm talking about? Good. I wish I did!

This is the problem with some exam subjects – you're asked to express views which are going to be read by a complete stranger, and you don't know whether what you write is going to upset this stranger or not. You don't know whether your point of view is going to be so different from theirs that they are going to get really cross and mark you down. It shouldn't happen. Exam markers are meant to be impartial. But they are human, more or less.[1] When you do essays for your own teacher you know how to adjust what you write in order not to upset her. You know her opinions, foibles and funny little ways. You know how to massage her ego, impress her by quoting stuff back at her that she's taught you. But none of these little tricks - and they *are* tricks - work on examiners. You don't know them, they don't know you, and this is just another pressure on you during an exam. So what do you do? Run screaming from the room? Twiddle your thumbs? Stare out of the window? You can do any or all of these things, but the best thing to do is this: write what you believe to be right, but you make sure that your reasons are very clear. Writing, "I think C.S. Lewis is rubbish. He wouldn't know a tree if it bit him on the leg," is probably not going to endear you to the examiner, unless you can support your argument by using quotes etc., to explain why you feel the way you do.

IN THE WORDS OF PROFESSOR A.L. ROWSE, "C.S. LEWIS IS RUBBISH- HE WOULDN'T KNOW A TREE IF IT BIT HIM ON THE LEG..."

1: Well they're teachers a lot of them, so it's less really.

The same applies to every subject: make sure that if you're saying something controversial, your reasoning is sound, or don't do it at all.

The waiting game

So let's assume that you've got through the exam period, which may have lasted a few weeks or longer, depending on what options you're taking, how much course work you've had to present, etc. Let's also assume that you behaved impeccably throughout the exams and didn't do anything likely to offend anyone.[1] You didn't break any of the rules, didn't eat, cheat or sleep in any exams. You were a model examinee. So what happens now? Well, obviously there's a period of going a bit mad, letting off steam, partying maybe, until it suddenly dawns on you – exams are about passing.

Yes, strangely enough nobody gets a prize just for turning up.

If you don't pass, you won't even get a certificate that says:

Dawn Scroggins Attended a two hour examination in Modern History
J.P.Sharkfrightener
CHIEF EXAMINER

If you got that, even if you failed, at least you'd be able to hang it on the wall so that everyone would know that you knew a thing or two about Modern History,

1: Although as you know this is almost impossible in any situation involving adults.

even if you didn't actually know enough to pass the exam.

Exams only mean something if you pass them. Which is why, while you wait for your results, you can go slowly out of your mind.

Which is probably the best place to be. After all, your mind during this period is so stuffed with *ifs* and *buts* that there's hardly room for you to be in there as well.

Unfortunately, once you've handed your paper in there's nothing you can do about it. It gets marked, warts and all. You can't change things. You can't even nip round to the examiner's house and explain that you hadn't meant to answer the same question twice, or write the entire paper backwards. You're stuck with it. And because of this there's really no point in worrying about it. Not that that's going to stop you!

Worry is all part of the exam process. You panic about not having done enough work, you get stressed about not understanding the questions, you worry about how badly you've done. It's normal. Stressful, but normal. It's also made worse by the fact that you've probably made some decisions about your future. You know roughly which exams you need to pass in order to become whatever it is you want to become, and (wouldn't you know it?) the very subjects that you need to pass are the very ones that you *just know* you've done really, really badly in! That's normal too. Not helpful, but normal.

Then you start to worry about grades. Let's assume that you want to go to sixth-form college, and you've been told that you need at least five grade "C" passes to get in. What happens if you get four Bs and a D? Will that count as five Cs? Would a couple of As help?

Who knows? You'll just have to wait and see!

Eventually the envelope drops through your front door. Or perhaps in your area the results go to your school and you have to go in and collect them. This is often a better way of doing things because it means that you get to know how well, or how badly, you've done before your parents do. That way if you've done well you can swagger home, toss the results casually on the table and say: "See? I told you so!" And if you've done badly you can leave the country! Of course if your results pop through the door then the chances of you getting to them before your parents are pretty slim. Mind you, the chances of your parents getting to them before the dog does are pretty slim too, so maybe there's not too much to worry about.

But let's assume that you get the results you want. "That's it then," you say. "I'm made for life."

And you walk off into the sunset.

Do you? Of course you don't! It doesn't end there. As I have said several times earlier, life is a series of tests, and just because you've done well in a few exams at the age of 16, there's no reason for you to sit back and think you've made it. What about "A" levels? University? College? An apprenticeship? What about all the other little tests life throws at you from now until the day you die? And even then there's probably a test to make sure you're actually dead and not just pretending in order to avoid talking to a nosy neighbour. No, I'm sorry to say it, but GCSEs are just a drop in the ocean. Testing and examination have only just begun.

Learning to cope...

Unfortunately, the tests that life throws at you vary from person to person, from job to job and from area to area,[1] unlike school, where there are particular tests at set times – which in theory should make them easier to avoid but in practice doesn't. So how do you cope? Well, you try to prepare yourself by having as many tricks and dodges up your sleeve as the thickness of your arm will allow. And this is where I come in. I have gathered together as much useful, useless and frankly pointless information as I think is necessary to get you through this particular aspect of life. When I say "I", I actually mean me and my hand-picked and steam-washed team of experts. Let's meet them!

Ombargo Appledorin
No team of experts would be complete without a know-all. And mine is Ombargo. Ombargo is a Doctor of Psychology. At a young age he realized the importance of "ologies". Frankly, anybody with an "ology" gets taken very seriously. Unless they've also got orange hair. And huge teeth. And a lighting-up bow tie. And a passion for doing chicken impressions. Sadly, Ombargo has all these things, but for all that I have to admit that he was an extremely useful member of my team. He had

1: Not to say country to country – although I just did.

77

skills that made him invaluable. For instance, he was particularly good at getting us thrown out of restaurants just before the bill arrived.

Phyllida Thribb

Every team also needs someone who's good at making coffee. This wasn't Phyllida. Her particular skill was looking disapproving, but she had been an Outside Examiner, and therefore I got her on to my team in the hope that she would provide some insights into the workings of the exam system. She didn't. She ate all the biscuits instead. What made things worse was the

fact that her examiner's training was so deeply entrenched that nobody was allowed to talk in her presence. This was tricky, because the only times we met were to discuss progress. In the end we took to passing notes, even though we knew that that wasn't allowed either. Gosh! Did we feel naughty!

Roger

Despite his incongruous name, Roger was a toy poodle. Well, actually he was a real poodle, but because of his size he was referred to as "toy". He was also referred to as "that damned dog" and "oi, dribbler!" He was not a popular member of the team, mainly because of his stupidity. I tried to point out to the others that it wasn't really his fault, that all dogs are stupid (they're born like it) but this just made matters worse. The only good thing about having him on the team was the fact that, because he was a toy poodle, he was able to get into places the rest of us just couldn't. Unfortunately we never needed to get into poodle parlours. We managed to use him for much of our undercover – or under-table – work. It was quite easy to hide a small camera

and microphone in the little fluffy bits he had – as all poodles do for some unknown reason – round his legs. We obviously had to be very careful when he was "wired up" in case he wee'd and blew himself up.

Mickey Shorthouse

Yes! My old school chum, as mentioned in previous *Coping With*... books. It was really nice to see him again after all these years, although I soon realized why we hadn't stayed in touch. He spent much of the time regaling us with tales of his schooldays. Unfortunately they were my schooldays too, and most of the stories seemed to involve me doing something

extremely childish and deeply embarrassing with bits of string.[1] The rest of the team thought he was brilliant; I thought he was the most convincing argument for bringing back the death penalty that anyone could possibly come up with.

These are the "experts". Obviously I didn't take them on without giving them a rigorous exam first. I've reprinted it here, just in case you should ever need to create your own team of experts:

1) Are you prepared to join my team of experts?
2) Are you prepared to do it without being paid?

That certainly sorted the wheat from the chaff.

What follows is the fruits of our "research", compiled into what I hope will be a useful guide to coping with the stresses and strains that exams and testing can put on you.

1: Don't even *try* to work it out, it's just too embarrassing, OK?

Coping with Exams & Tests – An A-Z

What follows is a mish-mash of facts, figures, jargon and other stuff designed to help you cope with any kind of test situation. It is arranged in alphabetical order for no reason other than the fact that it makes it easier to find what you're looking for. If it's there, of course. Bear in mind that this is by no means the definitive list – these are the results of the research of a bunch of ... sorry, I mean a carefully picked team of experts. Use it as you see fit!

A

"A" Levels (or Scottish "Highers")

Let's suppose you enjoyed your GCSEs so much that you want to do some more. Well, you can. You can stay on at school in the sixth form[1], or Years 12 & 13 just to confuse you, and take "A" levels.

Animal Testing

Although the name might suggest otherwise, this does not mean rabbits and hedgehogs sitting in rows of desks trying to prove how much they know about quantum physics. But perhaps it should. Certainly the animals would be a lot better off. Animal testing is a way of discovering whether drugs, disinfectant, shampoo, etc. are dangerous for humans.

WELL, I PREFER THE LAGER WITH THE WIDGET...

1: Or go to a separate sixth form college.

This is one form of testing that is probably less popular than GCSEs, if that's possible!

B

Bunking Off

Ah! This is more like it! Let's get away from "A" levels (and animal testing)! Let's get away from everything! Bunking off's the time-honoured art of dodging, or wagging school, playing truant or hookey.[1] This is quite a handy way of avoiding exams, if a very short-term one. You see, as I've mentioned earlier, exams can't really be avoided. If you're down to do one, then bunking off is only going to delay the agony. A bit like putting off going to the dentist. You may feel that you've avoided the pain of dental treatment, but the tooth still hurts. To be honest, if you've got an exam it's best to sit it the day you're supposed to. That way you get it over and done with.

Useless fact: bunking comes from the Old English *bunk* as in bed and *king* as in royalty, therefore "bunking off" means literally to lie around in bed all day like royalty. Probably.

C

Cheating

During our research we discovered many and various ways of cheating during exams, from having the answers written on your legs to having a small two-way radio receiver stuffed in your ear.

When I took Maths GCSE the one thing I could not get into my head was all those stupid formulae. So I spent ages carefully writing them on my ruler. Brilliant! No problem!

1: Not to be confused with playing hockey.

"Then you forgot to take it into the exam!"

That was Mickey Shorthouse chipping in without being asked. Typical! He's right, though. That's exactly what happened. But, do you know, afterwards I was pleased. I mean, suppose I'd been caught? That would have been the end of it. Kicked out of the exam without a chance to resit it! As it was, I remembered all the formulae and passed the exam, which I wouldn't have done if I'd been caught.

According to Miss Thribb the most extreme case of cheating she ever came across was a boy who left the exam on the pretext of having a stomach upset. He'd managed to fill the room with a foul-smelling green mist to add credibility to his claim.[1] He smuggled his exam paper out by shoving it down the back of his trousers (the last place anybody would want to look in the circumstances!) and then passed the paper over to a

1: Where the green mist came from is anybody's guess!

team of unemployed geniuses,[1] who answered the questions for him.

In order to avert suspicion about his absence he replaced himself with a remote-controlled model of himself made entirely from used matchsticks. He then smuggled the completed paper back under the pretext of being a singing Exam-O-Gram.

"What did the Examiner do?" asked Ombargo. "I would have thrown the book at him!"

In fact, that's exactly what the Outside Examiner (not Miss Thribb on this occasion) did. He threw the complete works of Shakespeare at the boy – or rather at the matchstick replica. The impact of the book demolished the side of the model's head, causing the Examiner to be arrested for manslaughter before he had time to discover that the "boy" was a fake. Justice was swift in those days. The upshot was that the boy passed his exam, only to be arrested some years later for setting fire to the school (his defence claimed that he needed the matches).

"What about the matchstick model?" asked Mickey, who never liked loose ends.

According to Miss Thribb the matchstick replica eventually married a teacher and became a school inspector.

1: The country's full of them.

Cycling Proficiency Test

The idea behind this test is to try and find out whether or not cyclists are safe on the road. Even if they're not, the examiners don't have the power to stop them cycling on the road. And if they are, the little badge they're given doesn't make them accident proof. So what's the point of it? Well, obviously it is a good idea to have your cycling skills tested, even if failure makes no difference to the person's access to roads. Anyone taking the test also gets instruction in how to care for their bike, for example:

Cleaning: Get your dad to do it.

They also get taught hand signals. Here are a few important ones:

I AM TURNING LEFT | I AM TURNING RIGHT | I AM FALLING OFF

D
Dates

The one thing that forces most students to give up history, apart from the fact that it can be incredibly boring, is dates. That's unfortunate, because history is all about when things happened. One of the ways of remembering dates is to make up little rhymes. The most famous is probably, "In fourteen hundred and ninety-two Columbus sailed the ocean blue." Or was it 1942? You see, that's the slight problem with this method of remembering dates – it doesn't work.

Driving Test

We all understand the basics of driving. We've watched our mum, cringed at our dad, or even had a go ourselves. But there comes a point at which, if we want to be let loose on the highways and byways of this planet, we're going to have to prove that we can do it. The Driving Test, as the test for driving is not surprisingly called, has become more complicated recently. This – we are told – is to try to reduce the number of cars on our roads. Why they can't just take one of those big crushing machines to them I don't know, but still.

Actually, the real reason that the test has got harder is because the people who organize it got annoyed that so many of us found it so easy to pass.[1] So they introduced a written section to the test, presumably remembering that the bit they hated most at school was the writing. This is rather strange because the one thing driving doesn't involve is writing. It involves decision-making, technical skill, orienteering, even the use of language – whether asking the way or yelling at other motorists – but nothing needs to be written down. The main reason

1: You might not believe this when you watch people drive, but it's true.

for this is because driving is essentially a two-handed job. But not the test apparently. Now you have to sit down and answer with your pen more or less the same sort of question you once answered with your mouth.

Is it going to make any difference to the breaking distance at 50 m.p.h. whether you write it or say it? Of course it isn't! If they wanted to make the test harder, why not do it blindfolded? Or with no petrol in the tank? Or just go back to the old test with its "I'd now like you to attempt a three-point turn without driving over any-body's garden," or "When I bang my head on the wind-screen you'll know that you've braked far too sharply."

No, that would be much too simple. And one thing you'll learn about this test-mad world we live in is that if it's simple, then forget it! It's got to be complicated and cause stress, otherwise it's a waste of time. Unfor-tunately, most of us want to get from "A" to "B"[1] by the most convenient method. And the most convenient method is still by car – which is why it's still the most popular, particularly if Dad's buying the petrol.

Dunce

An outdated term for somebody who's not doing so well at school. A standard was set, usually by continual

1: Or Accrington to Bognor.

testing, and anyone who didn't reach that standard was considered to be stupid. To make matters worse they were often made to wear a special dunce's cap, usually made out of a sheet of school paper. This paper became known as foolscap paper, because it was used to make a dunce's – or fool's – cap. The term has now gone out of fashion because everyone has realized (at last!) that people develop at different rates and are good at different things. For instance, I used to get into trouble at school because I couldn't (and still can't) spell. We seemed to have spelling tests every five minutes, so, as you can imagine, I was in trouble a lot! Fortunately I never had to wear a dunce's cap, because there were other things that I was good at.[1]

"No, there weren't!"

Keep out of this, Mickey!

E

Examiner

Who *are* these people? There are various types of examiner involved in making your life a misery by forcing you to sit exams. We've already met an Outside Examiner (more of them later), but there are also the people who actually set the questions, and the people who mark your answers to the questions. To understand why these people apparently take delight in your misery you have to know who they are. You've guessed it – teachers or ex-teachers! Either way they are people who have had their lives made miserable by some child, so they believe, and now they are getting their own back! Unfair? Of course it is! But then these are adults. Fairness doesn't come into it.

1: I can't remember what – but oh! There must have been!

Eye Tests

If you've never had an eye test, and some people haven't,[1] let me explain what it is. The optician puts you in a chair, and after shining a torch in your eyes so that he nearly blinds you, he puts some drops into them to finish the job. He then puts a machine so close to your eye that it nearly touches the back of your head.

"This," he explains, "is to test for glaucoma."

Why he can't just ask you if you've got it, I don't know. As far as I understand glaucoma is something you'd definitely know about if you had it. As if this isn't enough he then puts a pair of glasses on you and asks you to read a wall chart. Two things here: why put glasses on you if he doesn't know whether you need them or not? And why get you to read something that is clearly not in English? Have you seen those charts? They don't make any sense! For a start the spelling's appalling! *The* - T.H.A. - I ask you! Where do they get them from?

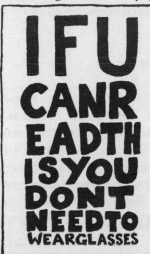

Whenever I have an eye test I just humour the poor bloke. Make something up. But it doesn't matter what I say it still ends up with him insisting that I need glasses. But then he *would* say that wouldn't he? After all he's an optician, and what do opticians do when they're not dribbling toxic chemicals on to people's eyeballs? That's

[1]: Although I'm sure we've all seen lots of football refs who need them!

right – they sell glasses. This is just one example of a test that is carried out simply to get you to buy something.

F
Failure

You should never think you've failed an exam, but rather that you haven't passed. Will this help? Probably not, because after all, the whole point of taking an exam is to pass it. That's what you work towards, what you worry about, what causes all the stress. The only encouraging thought is that you can always sit the exam again. And again. And again if necessary. Could you put yourself through all that? Neither could I!

G
Gifts

One of the best ways to pass an exam is to try to do well in it. One of the worst is to try to bribe the examiner with a little gift. They won't appreciate it. Apart from the fact that it's against the rules, examiners just aren't the kind of people who *ever* get gifts from anyone, and they won't know how to deal with the situation. Forget it – these people cannot be bought.

GM

This stands for "grant maintained" and refers to schools who have "opted out", which means that instead of being controlled by the local authority, they look after their own budget. Now this obviously means that they have to make sure that the school is popular, because the more pupils attending the school, the bigger the grant they get. And without a big enough grant the school would be forced to close.

This means that the school has to perform well in the local league tables, which means that its pupils have to be good at exams. But how does any of this affect you? Well, if you already go to a "GM" school, you're probably very aware of the pressure that you're under to do well. But if you're hoping to go to a "GM" school, then good luck! The competition is very fierce!

H
Higher Education

Something you can go for if you get really hooked on exams, because the higher you go up the education ladder, the more varied the range of exam choices there are. There are over 50 subjects that you can take at "A" level for a start, and that number just grows and grows. In fact you could stay in higher education for the rest of your life!

Homework

Homework is another form of testing. Since it's usually directly related to what you've been taught that day in school, it's the teacher's way of checking whether or not you've learned anything. The system falls down when the teacher doesn't mark the work immediately, because this means that they've gone on to teach you a new thing without checking that you've absorbed the last thing. Teachers and pupils should come to an arrangement. Pupils will look as though they've absorbed what they've learned (even if they haven't) in return for no homework. That would work, wouldn't it?

I
Incentives

Parents and others often try to get you to work harder at your various exams by offering incentives or bribes. It often starts in a really small way:

IF YOU DO WELL IN YOUR SPELLING TEST I'LL LET YOU WATCH 'BLUE PETER'

Or:

IF YOU DO BADLY IN YOUR SPELLING TEST I'LL MAKE YOU WATCH 'BLUE PETER'

These bribes increase in value as your tests and exams become more frequent. Some parents, not realizing just how many tests you get, find that by the time you get to GCSEs they're having to say things like:

ER...IF YOU PASS YOUR GCSES I'LL BUY YOU CORNWALL

The trick is to make sure that your parents don't offer you so much in incentives that they have to sell the house and go and live in a cardboard box.

The only downside of all this is that you have to keep passing the exams in order to win the prizes. But then you can't have everything, can you?

Initiation Ceremonies

These are often used by gangs and secret clubs to test new members. "Initiation ceremony" is just a posh name for entrance test. One gang I was once in would let you join if you could say "initiation ceremony" without getting a knot in the end of your tongue. But what do they consist of? Well, it rather depends how much the existing gang members want the new member to join. If they really want the new kid then they might make the initiation extremely easy – something like, "Say 'please' ". But if they don't want the newbie anywhere near them, they might say: "Cover a live polar bear in yeast extract and take it to the movies to see *Bambi*." Now that would be tricky, especially in somewhere like Coventry, where they haven't shown *Bambi* for ages. There's one main rule about initiation ceremonies – the person whose club it is can decide on the initiation. So if you want to be in a club but avoid the hassle, start your own!

Ink-blot Tests

If you've never had an ink blot test, let me explain what it is. Someone (presumably someone with a huge certificate to show that they are specially trained in the art of administering this test) shows you a series of pictures of ink blots. You then have to say what those ink blots remind you of. Here are a few examples:

THIS REMINDS ME OF A Messy ink Blot

THIS REMINDS ME OF A Small ink blot

THIS REMINDS ME OF A Splattery ink BLoT

The way in which you respond to these blots tells the expert all sorts of things about you – things they might tell you after giving you a very strange look. There is a way round this kind of test. When the "expert" says: "What does that remind you of?" say, "An ink blot". The logic of that really does their head in!

IQ Tests

IQ is the abbreviation for Intelligence Quotient. This is your tested mental age compared to your actual age. You've probably heard people being talked about as having a high IQ, which means that their mental age is higher than their actual age. It doesn't, unfortunately, follow that they'll be any good at exams. Somebody with a high IQ can be a complete dunce when it comes to getting a couple of "A" levels. But then IQ rather assumes that the intelligence you're born with is a fixed quantity and can't be altered or improved, even by being educated. This makes a bit of a nonsense of school really, doesn't it? And if school's a waste of time, then so are exams and testing! IQ sounds like a good thing to me!

J

Joined-up Writing

The thing we all struggle to master when we are young. It's also a great way of getting round not quite knowing the answer. What you do is put down something that you think looks about right, and then scribble in an apparently desperate attempt at joined-up writing. With any luck the examiner might be fooled into thinking that you've got the answer right and give you the marks. A word of warning though: this only really works until you're about seven!

K

Kindergarten

Testing is starting earlier and earlier these days. It even happens at kindergarten – or play group, play school, nursery or whatever else it's called. In some cases the word *rip-off* might be more appropriate, and this is probably why the government is sending their testers in to check on kindergartens. At least it would be nice to think that's why they're doing it – it's far more likely that they've just got the testing bug.

You may be wondering exactly what you can test a three- or four-year-old on that hasn't already been checked at the clinic. But these tests are not so much for the children, they're for the kindergarten leaders – those mumsy types who move about with a rustle of hand-made jumper and a strange clucking noise. So the kids aren't likely to be given a French aural or a calculus test – at least not for a couple of years.

WELL, MRS WIBLEY, THEY MAY BE VERY GOOD AT FINGER PAINTING, BUT THEIR GRASP OF QUANTUM PHYSICS IS FRANKLY PATHETIC!

L

League Tables

I mentioned these earlier and promised a bit more detail. I think they're worth looking at more closely because they are the things that cause more pain in education than anything else – except perhaps the caretaker's dog.

Since the introduction of the National Curriculum (covered in greater detail in a minute – be patient!) almost everything academic is now governed by league tables. But you'd be surprised how few people understand them.

So what are they? They're lists of schools, arranged in order of their success or failure, so that in theory you can tell at a glance whether or not the school that you go to, or the next school that you're *thinking* of going to, is any good. This presumably is so that you don't have to bother to have an opinion of your own. These lists are based on all sorts of data: GCSE results, "A" level results, SATs results and so on.

So why am I saying that they don't work? They don't work because the information in them is confusing. Let me give you an example. I know of a large secondary school in London – about a thousand pupils – whose league table results showed that every child who was tested in English achieved an above-average score. Brilliant, eh? Anybody looking at that would say: "Wow! That's the school to go to if I want to be good at English!" But what the league table doesn't tell you is that only *one* child in that school was tested in English, which is why in this instance the league table made no sense. But why should you worry about that? After all, league tables are for parents and teachers and the like, aren't they? Let them get on with it!

Well, yes and no. The problem for you is that if your school gets a bad press via the league tables, it reflects on all of its pupils.[1] It might even lead to parents – possibly *your* parents – going "up the school" and "having a go" at the teachers. That's the last thing you want, isn't it?

IT'S JUST NOT GOOD ENOUGH! IF YOU CAN'T DO BETTER NEXT TERM I'LL BE SETTING LINES FOR ALL OF YOU!

MUM!

LEAGUE TABLE

Useful fact: The best way to tell how good a school is, is to look not at its exam results, but at its level of absenteeism. If that's very high then it probably doesn't mean that the school has a lot of illness, but rather that the school has a lot of truancy. And if the pupils don't want to be there, it probably means it's not worth going to!

1: In the case of a "GM" school – as I mentioned earlier – this can be fatal.

98

Libraries

One of the big differences between exams and real life is *libraries*. Why? Because if you don't know something in real life you can look it up. If you don't know something in an exam you can fail.

Lie Detector Tests

You've probably seen these in films. Some dodgy-looking person – or even the hero or heroine – is strapped to a strange-looking machine and asked a number of questions by a strange-looking man in a white coat, in order to find out whether or not they're telling the truth. Throughout the ordeal they sweat a lot – probably because the straps are too tight. The person asks them a few simple questions to start with, just to check whether the machine is working, questions like, "What is your name?" "What did you have for breakfast?" Then they come in with the biggie, "Did you murder Mariella Gobstopper?" – assuming that this is what the *victim* is being accused of.

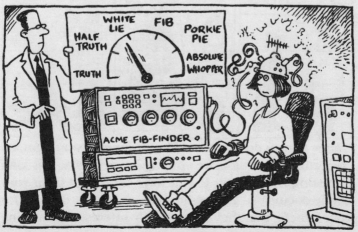

Obviously they don't ask that question if Mariella Gobstopper is alive and well and living in Pinner. The principle of the machine is that your heart rate, blood pressure and so on change when you lie. So by recording these things they can tell whether you're lying or not. Probably. Of course the system isn't perfect, because most people's heart rate automatically changes if they get strapped to a strange-looking machine by a strange-looking man in a white coat.

M

Medical Tests

There comes a time in everyone's school life when they have to take a medical. This is rather like giving you a test to make sure you're fit enough to face a firing squad. It's also one of the few chances adults at the school get to laugh at your underwear. Why you can't just bring in a note from your family doctor to say that you're fit I don't know. Well, I do actually.

If they let you do that they'd be throwing away a golden opportunity to humiliate you. And that's what this kind of testing is all about. If you have a medical from your family doctor you get the impression they're doing it for your benefit; that they're genuinely interested in making sure you're perfectly fit. The doctor's medical can be very reassuring – pleasant almost – as long as you haven't got anything wrong with you and the doctor hasn't got cold hands. Of course if you've got your parents with you then they talk to the doctor about you as though you're not there, but that's nothing – that's just the sort of stuff adults do. The school medical is a different kettle of fish, and in some extreme cases even involves kettles and fish. For one thing it's full of strange rituals, the purpose of which is never clear or explained. Boys for instance, are often told to "look out of the window and cough". I can only assume that this is to test whether coughing affects your eyesight. Whatever the purpose, the results are a bit hit and miss, mainly due to the fact that the doctor also has their (cold) hand down the front of your Y-fronts. All I've ever learned from that particular test is that coughing can make your eyes water.

Memory

The biggest single cause of exam stress is ... er ... what is it again? Oh yes! That's it – memory![1] However hard you study, however much you worry, if your memory gives out on the day, you're stuffed. But never fear, my team of experts have come up with a variety of ways to remember things.

THE BEST WAY TO REMEMBER THINGS IS TO TRY NOT TO FORGET THEM!

Er ... yes. Thank you, Ombargo. I'm sure that's very useful.

1: Sorry, I've just realized that I've done this memory gag before. I just can't remember where.

PERSONALLY I THINK THAT... WHAT WAS THE QUESTION AGAIN?

WOOF!

In fact my good friend – sorry, one-time friend – Mickey came up with a half-decent, if complex, method. This is only really useful if you're trying to remember a sequence of events or something similar, but this is it: Select the things you need to remember – dates, facts, etc. – and then attach a number to them. So if you're trying to remember 20 things in sequence, number them one to 20. Then think of an object that rhymes with the number, like this:

One · · ·

Two

Three

Four

Five

Six

Seven

Eight

Nine

Now all you need to do is to connect the object to the fact. For instance, let's imagine that you're trying to remember the order of the Stuart kings and queens. In this case you'd imagine Robert II eating a bun (1), Robert III tying his shoe (2), James I up a tree (3), James II opening a door (4), James III diving (5-ing) into a swimming pool, James IV making a fire out of sticks (6), James V as an angel in heaven (7), Mary eating a meal off a plate (8), and James VI down a coal mine (9). Simple!

Even simpler in my opinion (although I know this'll make Mickey sulk) is to remember that all Stuart kings were called James apart from two Roberts and a Mary. But maybe that's just too easy!

N

National Curriculum

I promised – or maybe threatened – to talk about it, and here goes! One of the big excuses that teachers use these days for teaching you unpleasant stuff is: "It's part of the National Curriculum." But what is the National Curriculum, and where did it come from?

Because of the way schools have developed over the centuries, there were a number of different things being taught in different areas. Obviously children were being taught to read and write at more or less the same age, but what about all the other things? What bits of History were they learning? Were they learning any at all? Or at least any that was of any use to them?

The other problem with the range of things being taught was that schools couldn't be checked up on. How could the authorities know whether anything was being taught? I suppose they could have just trusted the teachers, but weren't the teachers moaning about wanting more money, more resources and so on? Teachers aren't supposed to do that. They're supposed to shut up and teach, and if they've got time to whinge they clearly can't be doing that properly. Or so the argument went. Thus a system had to be created where everybody was taught the same things so that everyone – teachers, pupils, local education authorities, and especially teachers – could be checked up on at any time.

And so the National Curriculum was created, setting out exactly what had to be taught and when. But how did they do this? Did they sit around in a room and just pull a few ideas out of a hat? Of course not! We're talking about the education of generations to come! No, they consulted teachers, experts and educationalists. They gathered data, processed it, stored it and sifted it. And then they pulled a few things out of a hat. Not surprisingly it was a bit of a muddle at first, so they got the bloke who runs the National Lottery (he wasn't doing that then) to sort it out. And it's still being sorted. But it's also being taught. In fact it forms the basis of everything you do in school and every exam you sit. So now you know who to blame. Of course there is an upside. Because nobody has the foggiest idea what's on the National Curriculum, you can use it to get round your parents.

Might work.

Nerves

We all have nerves. They run all over our body, and are an essential part of the way our bodies work. So why is it that, at the time when you most need them to behave themselves, i.e. in the middle of an exam, they choose to go walkabout? At times like this people say: "I've got nerves." What they actually mean is that they haven't got nerves! The entire nervous system has upped and left for a two week holiday in another galaxy. Of course you don't need GCSE Biology, or the scout and guide equivalent (practical field surgery) to know that the nervous system can't actually leave the body. It makes a couple of good attempts, out of your bottom and out of your mouth, but it can't actually do it. So what it does is it finds a little corner to hide, in an armpit or something, and lies there whimpering pathetically: "Is the exam over yet?", and in the meantime you are on your own!

O

Outside Examiners

Outside Examiners are people occasionally brought into the school to make sure that no cheating takes place during the exam.[1] Why can't the teachers do this? Or the Head? Don't people trust them? If not, why haven't they been locked up? After all if they're good enough to teach you they should be good enough to examine you, shouldn't they?

Well, you would think so, yes, and in theory they are. But, as I've mentioned a few times, exams are not only about testing your abilities, they're also about testing your teachers too, which explains a) why your teachers

1: This applies more to selection exams than it does to GCSEs, although they can be used for those as well.

want you to do well, and b) why they're not allowed to supervise you sitting exams.[1]

Where do they come from? Somewhere that won't want them back in a hurry, that's for sure! There can't be a modern-day Dr Frankenstein somewhere building Outside Examiners out of badly-functioning body parts – can there? Well to be honest all the present evidence suggests that there might be. And perhaps he's being supplied by a small army of Burk and Hare-style bodysnatchers who hang around at the funerals of traffic wardens, park keepers and other suitably unsavoury candidates, in the hope of picking up a particularly black heart or strong stomach, both things you'd need for the job of Outside Examiner. The trouble is that these sorts of thoughts pass through your mind during the actual exam and you find yourself scanning them for visible signs of body-part surgery; a badly stitched wrist scar or a bolt through the neck. Don't bother. This will only waste your valuable writing time, and it's likely to count against you if they misinterpret your staring for flirting. What is more, you might find them hanging around the school gate waiting for you afterwards.

1: i.e. In case they help you cheat!

Of course the truth about these Outside Examiners is far less dramatic. In many ways you should pity them rather than loathe them. Try, for instance, to imagine them eating their lunch in the staffroom during midday break; chatting in a casual way with the lovely Miss Firmly, the newly appointed French mistress, or flirting harmlessly with Mr Hunt the Games master. What do you mean, you can't? Actually I'm not surprised, because it's unlikely that the Outside Examiner will be doing any such thing. It's far more likely that they've been spun some tale about the staffroom being out of bounds due to an outbreak of Mad Teacher's Disease. Either that or the minute the bell went the entire school staff including the Head locked themselves in the stationery cupboard.

After all, I don't know whether you noticed but as the Outside Examiner arrived in the playground even the caretaker's dog's tail went down, and this is an animal that once went 15 rounds with Bruno![1] Of course I'm not asking you to pity this person or even like them. After all, they choose to do this job. Nobody is forcing them. Neither is it a case of: "It's a nasty job but somebody's got to do it," because if nobody was prepared to do it the job wouldn't exist. But they are and it does.

1: Admittedly that was in pantomime but that can be tougher than the ring.

Overload

This is what can happen if you revise too much for an exam. You reach a point when not only can you not take any more information in, you also can't remember the stuff you've already revised. So how do you avoid overload? Easily! Don't bother to revise!

Panic

A direct result of overload. Another good reason not to revise!

Parental Choice

No, this doesn't refer to you being able to choose your own parents. Sadly that's still not possible, although with cloning ... who knows? *Parental choice* refers to the fact that your parents can choose which secondary school you go to. In theory.

This is how it works: your parents are asked to write down the names of three schools in order of preference. Preferably three schools that can be reached from your house by bus. They should be discouraged from putting down the name of some obscure Australian bush school, just because they'd read that Prince Philip once went there and they think that it made a man of him.[1] If your

1: Or that they think that it helped him marry the Queen.

parents don't know the names of three local schools I'm sure that a complete list can be obtained from the local education offices. To help with the choice, the local schools hold open evenings. They hide all the torture equipment and hang children's artwork over the bloodstains and invite parents and their children to wander freely around the school and ask any questions without putting their hand up or getting a detention.

Having studied the possibilities, your parents make their choices (or rather your choice for you) and then send the form off to the local authority. They then wait. And wait.

Eventually, assuming that none of the schools on the list gets burned down in the meantime, they'll get a letter back telling them that their child (you) has been selected to go to a *fourth* school that is not on the list and is almost impossible to enter unless accompanied by a platoon from the Special Boat Service. Now there is a reason for this, and it's not simply because parental choice doesn't actually exist, although that's a part of it. The reason is that the best school – the one at the top of your parents' (and everybody else's) list – is full. The second school on the list won't accept anybody who doesn't put them first. That's how snooty they are. And the third school is already full up with the kids who failed to get into the first and second ones.

So what can your parents do? Well, they can try appealing to the local authority. Although if your parents are like everybody else's they're unlikely to appeal to anybody, unless they put paper bags over their heads. There are about three stages of appeal, each one more complicated than the last, by which time you'll probably be too old to go to school anyway.

So why am I telling you all this? Because you will probably have sat an exam to get this far. You'll have sweated and revised and worried about your future, only to wind up going to the local dump. Just more proof of the pain of exams!

Parents

An even bigger cause of panic than overload. Unfortunately, they are also a good reason to ignore my advice about not revising, assuming you want a quiet life, that is!

Questions

The stuff that all exams are made of. This is the basic way of finding out whether or not you know something

– you get asked questions. The question you find your-self asking is: "Why am I putting myself through this torture?"

Quiz Shows

Quiz shows (or "game shows" as they are sometimes called) are just another form of exam. OK, so they're dressed up a bit to make them look like fun, but the bottom line is still that your ability to do or know some-thing is being tested, even if it's just how to balance a balloon while reciting a poem.

Of course it's rarely that simple, is it? Balancing a balloon while reciting a poem might be a bit embar-rassing, but it's not nearly humiliating enough for your average game show. Because they are tests in a funny hat,[1] game shows *have* to be humiliating; that's their job, just as it's the job of an exam or test to show you up. What's more, most game shows are designed to humiliate you in front of your mates.

AND NOW YOU JUST HAVE TO TRIM YOUR OWN HAIR WITH THIS CHAINSAW AND YOU WIN TONIGHT'S STAR PRIZE... A BOOK TOKEN!

You must have watched any number of quiz or game shows on kids' telly, where teams from different schools

---

1: OK – maybe not funny hat. But everything else is funny, except the presenter, which is a pity because they're the only thing that's *meant* to be funny!

111

compete against each other. Isn't there always one kid who can't get the answers right? And don't the rest of his/her team sigh heavily every time it happens? And doesn't the quiz master make things much, much worse by repeatedly saying, "It's not easy to think of the answer when you're in front of eight-and-a-half million viewers, you know!"?[1] Yes, well, that kid could be you or me! And probably would be!

And then there's *Family Fortunes*. Not only is it hideous to watch, but if you were fool enough to take part in it, it would also mean humiliation in front of your entire family, including that cousin you've always fancied. Do you think any of them are ever going to speak to you again if it's your fault that they fail to win the dream family holiday to the Costa Absolutely-nothingcosyou'vejustwonityoudumbos? Of course they won't! Mind you, that could be a good thing, but it doesn't alter the fact that game shows are just tests with sitting-behind-desks factor greatly reduced, only to be replaced by a much bigger humiliation factor. So if any of your mates or family suggest going on a game show, just tell them that you're too busy studying for GCSEs. Believe me, they're the easy option!

Quotations

If you get stuck in any test or exam – and you *will*, believe me – the way out is to bung in a quotation. It works wonders, buys you thinking time and gets you extra points.

"As the great philosopher, Marcel Proust, once said, 'It's a long nose that has no turning.'"

See? I bet you're really impressed. Of course it doesn't

1: Eight-and-a-half million? He should keep adjusting that figure, because every time he makes that stupid remark about it not being easy half-a-million viewers turn off.

work for every subject, although it might. Technical drawing for instance:

"The following cross-section has been drawn with a 2B pencil. As Prince Hamlet said: '2B or not 2B – that is the question.'"

Try it. You never know!

R
Revision

Another term for study. Revision basically means reminding yourself of something you already know. But all too often you find yourself saying: "I don't remember learning this!" To make things worse this usually happens when you're scanning your own notebooks! Aagh! That *is* scary! An entire project that you have absolutely no recollection of doing! You got a merit mark for it as well! It's at times like these that you really start to panic about exams!

Romantic Compatibility Tests

These take many forms, and are designed to help you find the boy/girl of your dreams. Unfortunately they're also designed to cause you maximum embarrassment.

Take the ones in magazines. You know the sort of thing: a list of multiple-choice questions to help you to *"Discover the Hunky Hot-Lips (or Luscious Love-Babe) lurking beneath that rather sad exterior of yours "*. These magazines never mince words.[1] You fill it in then check your answer against a *"How badly did you do?"* bit at the bottom of the page. You quickly realize that it doesn't matter what answers you choose, your chances of ever attracting anyone other than next-door's cat are non-existent.

But there's another problem. You knew there would be! It really doesn't matter how much you disguise your handwriting, the magazine is specially designed to fall open at the page with the questionnaire on it the minute anyone you fancy walks in the room. It's also designed to ensure that, however you try to disguise it, your handwriting is instantly recognizable! How do they do it? Who knows? But all I do know is that if you're ever tempted to fill out one of those things it will return to haunt you time and time again.

S

SATs

SATs – which you may remember stands for Statutory Attainment Targets – are the sharp end of the National Curriculum. They're the testing bit. What the National Curriculum does is to set out not only what must be taught, but at what age the pupils must know it. Some-

---

1: They never mince anything, actually. Except on the recipe page.

body sat down and worked out, for instance, that a child of five should know basic colours and be able to hold a pencil, but by the time they get to seven they should be able to design and build a nuclear power station. Or something like that. Any child who can't do it is failing, or the teacher is failing, or the school is failing – somebody's failing anyway (apart from the people who thought up the whole stupid business in the first place)!

These SATs form the basis of league tables which, as I explained earlier, don't make a lot of sense. As if learning wasn't hard enough without being told what you had to know and when you had to know it. And you get an extra test to boot!

Scouts and Guides

The scout and guide movement is another thing that could be a lot more fun if testing and exams hadn't crept in to spoil it. I'm sure that when Lord Baden-Powell (or "Uncle Bobby" as he probably was then) first thought up the idea during the Boer War he was thinking more along the lines of sitting round a camp-fire singing totally pointless songs and whittling a pointy stick. I doubt that he thought anyone would want to be tested on anything.

This testing is what scouts and guides refer to as "badge work". This is not to be confused with "badger work", which is something else entirely.[1] Now, there are probably people who will argue that there's no finer sight than a scout or guide marching along tilted sideways. This of course has nothing to do with a near-fatal tent-pole accident, but is caused by the bucket-load of badges attached to their shirt sleeve.

1: It involves badgers, cooking oil, and tossed salad. A good scout can cook anything.

They've got badges for everything: cooking, reading, stamp collecting, and virtually every bodily function. These poor kids have been tested for everything except drugs.[1]

LOOK! I GOT MY NEEDLEWORK BADGE!

The big question is – why? If one of those first boy scouts had said to B-P: "Sorry, Uncle Bobby, but I can't crawl through enemy lines risking life, limb and dirty knees tonight – I've got to study for my needlecraft badge," what do you think B-P would have said in reply? "Dib Dib," probably.

Set Texts

One of the major features of English Literature exams is the *set text*. This is a book that you have to read and be able to answer questions on. And not easy questions like "What colour was the heroine's hat?" either. It's usually hard stuff like "Discuss the use of metaphor in Chapter Four". I bet you didn't even know there *was* a chapter four, did you? You gave up on page seven!

Where do they get these books from? Well, my research suggests[2] that the examining body send someone to a bookshop to ask:

1: That doesn't normally happen until he gets into the Ranger Scouts.
2: Or at least Roger the poodle followed an examiner into a bookshop. Unfortunately he got thrown out for doing a poo in the corner. The examiner that is – not Roger.

And so it is that you have to study the worst book in the world (or Shakespeare – he's very popular for exams. Well, let's face it, he's *got* to be popular somewhere). Why can't they give you a set text that you really want to read? Like ... er ... well, like anything other than *A Passage to Bognor*!

Student

It sounds slightly romantic to say: "I'm a student," because it suggests that you're trying to better yourself intellectually. The fact that you may be ten and are only going to school because if you didn't your parents might get locked up is neither here nor there.[1] Students are the intellectuals of the future. They can have student rail cards, student grants, student loans. They can get into the theatre cheaper than lesser mortals. All they have to do is flash their student card and they can watch *Babes in the Wood*. A very good reason for leaving school as soon as possible, I reckon!

1: Really? Wow! That's the best reason for becoming a student I can think of!

Swimming Tests

Now before anybody says, "I do those!" let me say that I don't think there's anything wrong in wanting to learn to swim or to be tested for doing it. Let's face it, who wouldn't want the world to know that they could swim two miles butterfly?[1] Or pick a half-brick up off the bottom of the pool without clonking themselves on the side of the head with it? Or swim three lengths in their pyjamas?

These are all skills that will come in very useful in later life. Possibly. And there's nothing wrong with being proud of your abilities. There's not even a lot wrong with the occasional bit of boasting, as long as it's only occasional. When it *is* wrong – in my humble opinion[2] – is when people are made to feel that they have to push themselves, to be tested to the limit, in order to keep up with other people who are probably better at a particular thing than they are. This can be dangerous in any sport; and can be even trickier if it's happening under water.

IT'S PERFECTLY SIMPLE ANGELA – JUST SWIM DOWN AND PICK UP THE BRICK!

1: Butterflies can't swim, but swimming coaches don't seem to have realized this.
2: Regular readers will know by now that my opinion is *never* humble!

Swot

Swotting means revising, but there are actually two forms of the word. There's the verb to *swot*, as in I swot, you swot, that kid over there in the specs probably swots, etc. This is a GOOD THING. There is also the noun *swot*, as in "He or she is a swot". That is a BAD THING. You can swot without becoming a swot. Swots are obsessive. They feel that unless they go over and over and over stuff they'll never know it. Rubbish! You already know it – all you're doing when you swot is reminding yourself of  something you have already learned. As I said earlier in the book, exams – all exams – are about testing you on something you already know. Don't forget that. So swot. Don't *become* a swot. Thank you.

T

Teachers

Teachers can make or break your exam chances. They know what you're going through, after all. They've seen it before. They've been there themselves. The average teacher has probably done more exams that you've had exam panic attacks, which should make them sympathetic, shouldn't it? It should. It doesn't.

U

University

This is the ultimate in student cred. "I go to university, you know," sounds really good. Universities conjure up pictures of towns with medieval towers, girls on bicycles, musty books and people who look intelligent.

It's easy to forget that university has a downside. University students are forced to wear army surplus anoraks, drink revolting cider and listen to really obscure pop music.[1] If they're really unlucky Sir Paul McCartney will bring a band of ageing rock stars to do an impromptu pop concert in the student hall. And as if that wasn't bad enough, you actually have to study! Lots!

V

"Varsity"

Universities (or "Varsities" as they are sometimes called) are very competitive, and so are the students. If they're not trying to be cleverer than everybody else, they're

1: What do you mean you've never heard of Ozric Tentacles?

trying to beat them at football, rugby, rowing or marbles. The "Varsity" boat race for example, in which Oxford and Cambridge take part, is a big annual event in the university calendar. It even gets televised. Millions of people (who normally wouldn't touch rowing with a barge pole) tune in to see whether or not one of the boats sinks.

I HATE RACING THE SCIENCE DEPARTMENT

It's because of this competitiveness that many universities, particularly in America, are prepared to offer places to students who have physical, rather than mental, abilities.

"He may not be able to write his name – but gee! – he's a great quarterback!"

This is the cry heard in many a varsity principal's office.[1] But before you start thinking: "Yeah! That's how

1: "Principal" is maybe not the right word. Unprincipled would be a better one.

I'll get into University!", you need to be aware of the fact that using this method of extending your student life depends on two things: just how bad your "A" level (or Highers) passes were, and just how desperate the university is to fill its empty places. Oh, and just how much your parents are prepared to donate to the university building fund. Three things. Four if you count the fact that you need a real sporting skill – no university is likely to be impressed by your pog-playing prowess.

"Well Done!"

This may be all you want to hear after months of sweat and study. It can make the whole thing worth it.

"Well – Never Mind. Better Luck Next Time."

That is definitely *not* what you want to hear after months of etc., etc. It might be a good idea to warn your parents of this simple fact before they open their mouths and put their feet in!

Xams

If your spelling is as bad as this, maybe higher education is not for you!

Year Out

Many students, having got through the trauma of "A" levels, take a year out before deciding what to do next. This is another way of saying that they are going to have a year without study, without exams. And why not? They've earned it. But before you start thinking: "Brilliant! That's what I'll do!", it's as well to realize that nobody is likely to agree to you taking a year out after your Cycling Proficiency Test!

Z
Zeal

Something you need plenty of if you want to succeed in the competitive world of exams. Of course you may be like most of us, just wanting to get the exam results that you need to pursue your chosen career. In that case the thing you'll need probably begins with "L" – LUCK!

Aftermath

Not to mention After-Eng, After-Geog, After-Hist, and so on. Let's assume that you've done your exams, you've got the kind of results that you want, and you're all set up for the future. It's been hard work. It always is. Even my team of experts have had to exert themselves.[1] But then even they realize that if something is worth achieving it's worth working for. Oh yes, I know that I implied earlier that the team was thrown together with the scantiest of testing procedures, but I think it only fair that I should now reveal the truth.

Hand-picked and run under the tap

My team of experts were only put together after the most thorough and heart-searching examination, and even then only after spending a weekend at a conference centre,[2] where we underwent rigorous aptitude and self-assessment testing. This is my diary of events, which I think demonstrates the kind of commitment we were prepared to give to what we considered to be a very worthy cause.

Day One:
19.00 hours: We are inside what will be our "home" for the next 48 hours. We take anti-depressants. Several pints later it doesn't look so bad.
23.00 hours: We decide to have an early night as we have a long day ahead of us. I

1: Just putting the kettle on was a strain for Mickey.
2: Well actually it was the local day centre, but a couple of my team are not allowed out without supervision.

124

have worked out a bed-sharing rota beforehand to save arguments. It doesn't, and so we leave Roger to it and all curl up on the floor.

Day Two:
07.00 hours: We start our first "Self-assessment sharing session". This takes the form of breakfast, and with only one cereal bowl, two cups and a pair of sugar tongs, sharing is a must. It's situations like these that will really test the team's abilities. And stress levels.

10.00 hours: We finally settle down to our first self-assessment test. This is a fictitious survival problem. We have to pretend that we have crashed our plane in the desert. We have been given a list of a number of potentially useful items that we have supposedly salvaged from the plane before it exploded. Among the list of items are a mirror, some salt tablets, three back copies of *Just Seventeen* and a harmonica. I think that some of these things may be more useful than others. But where is our facilitator? We're supposed to have an outsider who coaxes and encourages us. Without that it is going to be hard to make a start. But we try anyway.

12.00 hours: We still can't agree on which desert we're supposedly stranded in. Phyllida and Ombargo say the Sahara, but Mickey says the Atlantic. Unfortunately he was away when we did Geography at school, and this gap in his education is beginning to show. Roger, incidentally, says "Woof!"

13.00 hours: Our facilitator finally arrives. He

125

apologizes for being late and explains that he had a rather "heavy night" yesterday.

17.00 hours: We finally solve the plane crash exercise, with Geoff's help. He doesn't actually say much, but we soon get to understand his little hints, such as banging his head on the table and screaming: "I've never met such a bunch of complete morons!" I think he likes us.

19.00 hours: To prevent a fight breaking out, Phyllida suggests that we stop for a bite to eat. Geoff suggests that we eat out and blow the expense. He obviously has no intention of paying. He knows this little Real Ale place that does nice bar snacks.

0004.00o bhoiurrss: we get bak frijm m the…

Day Three:

12.00 hours: After a shaky start we are planning to spend what's left of the day involved in an exercise designed to test our management skills under stress.

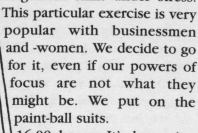

This particular exercise is very popular with businessmen and -women. We decide to go for it, even if our powers of focus are not what they might be. We put on the paint-ball suits.

16.00 hours: It's becoming fairly obvious that you should never cut corners where paint-ball is concerned. We're beginning to realize why they use the expensive special paint-ball washable paint, and not the cheaper industrial high-gloss from B&Q. We might also have chosen a less striking colour than luminous purple. Geoff seems to think that a good soak in a bath of white spirit might help, although it may take a week or two.

18.00 hours: We gather for our assessment session, which Geoff – as our facilitator and *critic friend* – will run. There is a long silence while Geoff stares ahead and we hang on to his every sigh. He seems uncertain where to start his assessment. He apologizes for having not made any notes, but having his hands welded together with luminous purple paint has made it a bit tricky to hold a pencil.

19.00 hours: As I stand on the steps of our weekend retreat, waving to my departing team, I marvel that a group of people with so few formal qualifications[1] should be able to blend and meld into such a crack investigative force. And I do mean crack. As Phyllida struggles to cycle up the road, the bottom half of her body one large crusty paint-ball, I just know that between us we are going to be able to seek out the answers you need in order for you to be able to cope with exams.

1: Few but not none. I have two GCSEs and a cycling proficiency certificate. Ombargo has a black belt, which really clashes with his brown shoes, Phyllida has been a teacher so she must have some qualifications, although not necessarily. Mickey can juggle and Roger has won Crufts. Well, not actually won, but he's been out with a winner. Well, not actually "out" – he gate-crashed her kennel one night.

School's out

So let's assume that all my team's hard work and effort was worth it, and you are now standing at the threshold of your future with a bucket-load of qualifications. Yes! You are ready, willing, and fully able to step out on to the highway of life.

Well, the High *Street,* anyway. As least I think it is. Let's ask somebody.

"Excuse me. Do you know whether this is the High Street?"

"I certainly do. But do *you* know the chemical formula for Hydrogen Peroxide? Or the capital of Rwanda? Or the name of the Limping Man in A.J. Plunkett's novel *Hands Off That Liver Pâté!*? Or the—"

YOU MAY NOW STOP READING.
PLEASE CLOSE YOUR BOOKS.